COMMONWEALTH OF
TOIL

COMMONWEALTH OF
TOIL

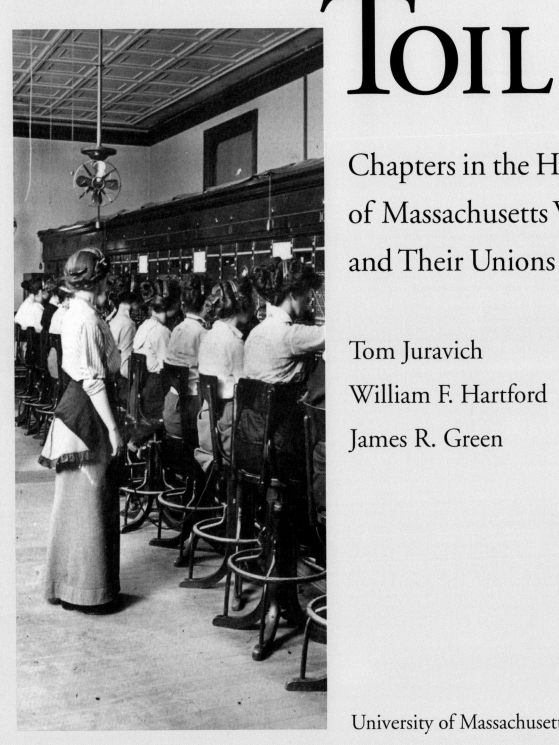

Chapters in the History
of Massachusetts Workers
and Their Unions

Tom Juravich

William F. Hartford

James R. Green

University of Massachusetts   *Amherst*

Copyright © 1996 by
University of Massachusetts Press
All rights reserved
Printed in the United States of America
LC 96-19249
ISBN 1-55849-045-0 (cloth); 046-9 (pbk.)

Designed by Dennis Anderson
Set in Adobe Garamond
Printed by Cayuga Press, Inc.

Library of Congress Cataloging-in-Publication Data

Juravich, Tom.
    Commonwealth of toil : chapters in the history of
Massachusetts workers and their unions / Tom Juravich, William F.
Hartford, James R. Green.
            p.   cm.
    Includes bibliographical references and index.
    ISBN 1-55849-045-0 (cloth : alk. paper). — ISBN 1-55849-046-9
(pbk. : alk. paper)
    1. Labor movement—Massachusetts—History. 2. Trade-unions—
Massachusetts—History. 3. Labor—Massachusetts—History.
4. Working class—Massachusetts—History. I. Hartford, William F.,
1949– . II. Green, James R. 1944– . III. Title.
HD8083.M4J87 1996
331.88'09744—dc20   96-19249
                                                CIP

British Library Cataloguing in Publication data are available.

For the working men and women of
Massachusetts, past and present

Commonwealth of Toil

We have a glowing dream

Of how fair the world will seem

When each one lives their life secure and free

When the earth is owned by labor

And there's joy and peace for all

In the Commonwealth of Toil that is to be.

Popular IWW song written by
Ralph Chaplin, 1918

Contents

Acknowledgments

A GREAT NUMBER OF PEOPLE HAVE MADE THIS book possible. We would first like to thank Robert Haynes, Secretary-Treasurer of the Massachusetts AFL-CIO. Bob originally came up with the idea for this project and has provided important support throughout the process. We also want to thank State Senator Thomas Birmingham, who was crucial in securing the funds from the state legislature that made this book possible. To both of them we are deeply indebted.

Introduction

MASSACHUSETTS HAS AN EXTRAORDINARY history of work and labor. It was in mill towns such as Lowell, Lynn, and Lawrence that the modern factory system began. And these communities, as well as many other towns and cities across the Commonwealth, were sites of struggles that were central in the development of the American labor movement. Many important labor organizations, including the Knights of St. Crispin, the Women's Trade Union League, and Nine to Five, got their start in Massachusetts. For others, such as the Knights of Labor, the Industrial Workers of the World, and the American Federation of Labor, events in Massachusetts became formative parts of their history. From the Bread and Roses strike in Lawrence, through the struggle at the Colonial meatpacking plant, to recent victories at hospitals and universities, Massachusetts workers and their unions have been in the forefront of the fight for dignity and justice.

As a result of these struggles and the organizations they built, Massachusetts workers gained many important advances that would later be enjoyed by other American workers. The right to organize, restrictions on work hours and child labor, and workers' compensation were all pioneered in the Commonwealth. While it took several generations for these early experiments to become a reality for all workers across Massachusetts and the nation, they sprang from a vision of a better world.

This book contains eighteen chapters of this extraordinary and complex history. These are pieces of the quilt made by the people who struggled in what was for them the Commonwealth of Toil. From the outset we make no claim to provide readers with a complete history. We believe we have carefully chosen which stories to tell, yet there are many wonderful tales that remain untold. Space has also not allowed us to include material from a number of rich writings about Massachusetts social history, including working-class communities, family life, ethnic and race relations, and a number of other issues.

This volume is intended to be an introduction to the history of work and labor—to the people and the events that shaped what Massachusetts and the nation would become. It is a history too often ignored at both the high school and college level. We hope to have filled a gap for students as well as the general public. Most important, we hope to provide Massachusetts workers the opportunity to understand and celebrate their own history.

The project was coordinated at the Labor Relations and Research Center at the University of Massachusetts, Amherst with the assistance of the Center for Labor Research at the University of Massachusetts, Boston. This book is a collaborative effort of the three primary authors and a number of researchers and advisers. Patricia Reeve from the University of Massachusetts, Boston and Nancy Lessin from the Massachusetts Coalition for Occupational Safety and Health (MassCOSH) read early drafts and provided important comments and suggestions for revision. A number of people wrote first drafts of the sidebars including Jay Armstrong, Ted Chambers, Erin Enwright, David Glidden, and Jack McGlinn from the Labor Relations and Research

Center at the University of Massachusetts, Amherst, and Michael Bonislawski and John Cashman from the Boston College graduate history program.

Erin Enwright coordinated the photographic research for the project. This project would not have been possible without the efforts of individuals and institutions that worked with us identifying the photographs in this volume. We would especially like to thank: Linda Seidman, Ute Bargmann, Michael Milewski, and the staff in the labor archives at the W.E.B. Du Bois Library at the University of Massachusetts, Amherst; Paul Graves at the Holyoke Public Library; Aaron Schmidt at the Boston Public Library; Martha Mayo at the Center for Lowell History at the University of Massachusetts, Lowell; Ken Skulski at Immigrant City Archives in Lawrence; Elizabeth Mock, Healey Library Archives,

University of Massachusetts, Boston; and Ferd Wulkan, Susan Phillips, and Mark Erlich. We are grateful to all those who contributed to this project. We also would like to thank all the authors upon whose work we relied to tell these stories. Without their pathbreaking efforts this book would not have been possible.

Special thanks need to be given to Beth Berry of the Labor Center at the University of Massachusetts, Amherst. As the editorial assistant on this project, she tirelessly worked through many drafts of this volume. Her skill, patience, and good cheer helped make this book possible. We also would like to thank Bruce Wilcox and the staff from the University of Massachusetts Press. From our very first conversation Bruce was excited about this project and has been a tireless supporter throughout.

COMMONWEALTH OF
TOIL

PART I

WORKERS IN THE NEW COMMONWEALTH, 1800-1849

THE WORKING PEOPLE OF MASSACHUSETTS played a central role in shaping a revolution against the British Empire. From the 1747 riots against the Royal Navy's attempts to "impress" colonists into forced labor, to the revolt against the Stamp Act in 1765, to the Boston massacre of 1770 and the Boston Tea Party of 1773, Bay State workers initiated many of the stirring events that led to the nation's independence, and they played key roles in seeing those events to their conclusions.

A generation later, Massachusetts working people also played a central role in shaping the Industrial Revolution. These men and women left their farms to toil in the first textile mills created by the Boston Associates in Waltham and Lowell. They built the furniture, forged the iron, and labored as craftsmen in shops from North Adams to the North End of Boston. They were the labor power that generated America's Industrial Revolution.

But they were much more than just labor power. As they confronted kinds of work and types of employers that had not existed in the Bay Colony of their fathers and mothers, their struggles helped to define the world their sons and daughters would inherit. For the Industrial Revolution was not just forged by the industrialists and machines that together at times seemed to devour the human spirit. It was also being shaped by the defiance of Massachusetts workers who fought and struggled for dignity and justice.

The first industrial workers in the nation came from the farms of New England to towns such as Lowell in the 1830s. They had no experience with factories or cities, and no experience working at machines for wages. But the Lowell "mill girls" brought with them a proud heritage of independence gained in making a revolution against the British Empire a generation before. Even though they lacked the rights of citizens, these young women, these "daughters of free men," acted like citizens of a democratic republic as they confronted their employers. These Lowell textile-mill women knew nothing about labor unions, but they discovered the need for collective action as they formed a sisterhood of toil. In protesting wage cuts in their "turnouts," or what were later to be called strikes, and in demanding a ten-hour workday, the Lowell "mill girls" gave birth to a labor movement that sought social justice and economic security. They also began the struggle for women's rights in the workplace that still continues.

While considerably less dramatic than the change caused by the new mills of the Boston Associates, a fundamental shift occurred among craftsmen in workshops across the Commonwealth and the nation. In the colonial era, established masters, such as the famous patriot Paul Revere, owned their shops and employed journeymen helpers along with young apprentices. Many apprentices rose through the ranks to become masters who owned their own shops and employed others. By the 1820s, however, increased competition, larger-scale production, and the growing use of technology relegated many highly skilled workers to a future as lifelong wage workers. In many occupations, the craft skills that set artisans apart from common laborers were being eroded by these changes and the increasing use of machinery.

At the same time, the casual workplace of the earlier era disappeared. At one time the workday, largely under the control of workmen, had been punctuated by regular breaks, during which masters often joined journeymen in a few bowls of rum. A growing proportion of employers now embraced a new industrial morality that stressed hard work, temperance, and self-discipline.

In this context, the journeymen began to express their own interests, as opposed to those of the masters. They even struck against their own masters and asserted their desire for liberty from their employers. A new language appeared. Masters became "bosses" and journeymen became "hands." When the hands formed a fist and struck their bosses, employers went to court and judges issued injunctions against the strikers, who were accused of forming "criminal conspiracies" against the masters. Between 1806 and 1843, charges of criminal conspiracy were lodged against labor unions in six states on twenty-three separate occasions.

But workers refused to submit to what they called "judicial tyranny." They continued to assert their freedom of association, which they argued had been promised in the Bill of Rights. Their struggle came to a head in Massachusetts in the Bootmakers' case, *Commonwealth v. Hunt*. Chief Justice Shaw's 1842 decision recognized that the old English Common Law which bound servants to masters would not suffice in a free republic where workingmen enjoyed the rights of citizenship. Employers would still continue to use the law against unions, but bootmakers in Massachusetts had forced the courts—for the first time in the nation—to acknowledge the legitimacy of trade unions. It was one of many blows the Commonwealth's workers would strike to extend the liberty they had struggled so hard to win from the British.

By the 1840s, the expansion of the factory system in Massachusetts, the cutthroat competition among manufacturers, and the increased use of machinery led to work "stretchouts" and wage cuts. Yankee "mill girls" living in boardinghouses had been joined by poverty-stricken Irish families living in tenements. At the same time, the old "community of interest" between master craftsmen and journeymen had broken down. Many found their trades threatened by machines and factories and by unskilled "greenhands" who worked for poverty wages.

Here began a century of struggle for freedom from the tyranny of working from sunup to sundown six days a week. It began with the Boston carpenters' strike in 1825 for the ten-hour day and the campaigns of the Lowell Female Reform Association. It continued with the strikes of workers in the Charlestown Navy Yard and climaxed in the May Day general strike for the eight-hour day in 1886. Massachusetts workers led the nation in fighting for the humane working day, and no one articulated this demand better than Massachusetts workers such as Seth Luther, Sarah Bagley, and Ira Steward, who spoke for others who wanted to "work to live," not "live to work."

Bound up in their struggle was their concern for children who labored like adults in this commonwealth of toil. Robbed of their childhoods, their health ruined and their spirits broken, these girls and boys of the Commonwealth bore more than their share of the costs of the emergence of a new indus-trial order. And although their pain and suffering would continue far too long in Massachusetts and across the new nation, by 1842 the struggles of child workers helped persuade the Massachusetts legisla-ture to pass the first law limiting child labor, an important first step.

Throughout the 1830s and 1840s, workers in Mas-sachusetts and around the country remained insular. Yet they were being brought together by their loss of skill, the tyranny of the factory system, and what many felt was a drift away from the democratic ideals of the Revolution. And while their fledgling efforts at organizing did not prevail, their legacy did.

Two of the many young women working in the mills of Lowell, dressed in their work smocks.

CHAPTER I

Working Women and the Factory System in Lowell

THE LOWELL MILLS WERE AN IMPOSING SIGHT. To the young women coming from the farms of Massachusetts to work there, they were unlike anything they had seen before. On the outside they were massive stone and brick structures that towered over even the largest New England barn. Inside they were overwhelming. As one woman recalls her first day, "How was I filled with surprise at the sight presented to my view! Thousands of spindles and wheels were revolving, the shuttles flying, the looms clattering, and hundreds of girls overseeing the buzzing and rattling machinery! I looked into the various rooms, and saw all I wished for that time, and turned away, thinking for a moment I was deaf, and would never hear again. I thought I should never want to work in such a dangerous place as that."

But they did. And once the wonder passed, they found that mastering the machine they were assigned was frustrating and painful. This was especially true in weave rooms, where workers tended looms that wove yarns together according to a specified pattern.

She felt afraid to touch the loom, and she was almost sure that she could never learn to weave; the harness puzzled, and the reed perplexed her; the shuttle flew out and made a new bump upon her head; and the first time she tried to spring the lathe, she broke out a quarter of the threads.

That evening, as she left the mill,

There was a dull pain in her head, and a sharp pain in her ankles; every bone was aching, and there was in her ears a strange noise, as of crickets, frogs, and jews-harps, all min-gling together; and she felt gloomy and sick at heart. The day appeared as long as a month had been at home.

The experiences of the women who went to Lowell tell the story of the making of an industrial working class in America. As they left the farm villages where most of them had grown up, these women embarked on an adventure in which they would both challenge popular conceptions of women's roles in society and begin to define the rights of industrial workers. In the process, their exertions and struggles made them every bit as much pioneers as their westward-moving brothers on the nation's expanding agricultural frontier.

They were entering a strange and unfamiliar world, and few could conceal their initial fears. Harriet H. Robinson, whose mother ran a Lowell boardinghouse and who witnessed the arrival of many of these young women, left a memorable description.

When the large covered baggage-wagon arrived in front of a block of the corporation, they would descend from it, dressed in various and outlandish fashions, and their arms brimful of bandboxes containing all their worldly goods. On each of these was sewed a card, on which one could read the old-fashioned New England name of the owner. And sor-rowful enough they looked, even to the fun-loving child who has lived to tell the story; for they had all left their pleasant country homes to try their fortunes in a great manufacturing town, and they were homesick even before they landed at the doors of their boarding-houses.

Just five years after the ground had been broken for the first mill, Lowell was already a bustling center

Constructing one of the many canals that run through Lowell.

of activity. Captain Basil Hall wrote of an 1827 visit: "Several school-houses were pointed out to me, and no less than three churches; besides innumerable boarding-houses, taverns, newspaper offices, watch-makers, book-shops, hatters, comb-makers, and all the family of Stores, every one of them as fresh and new as if the bricks had been in the mold but yester-day." By 1833, the town had 12,000 inhabitants, 3,800 of whom were mill women, and nineteen five-story factories. At midcentury, Lowell would be the nation's foremost cloth producer and the second largest city in Massachusetts.

Compared with women already in Lowell, the new arrivals no doubt felt out of place. Many brought a rural dialect from the countryside. "On the broken English and Scotch of their ancestors," Harriet Robinson observed, "was ingrafted the nasal Yankee twang; so that many of them, when they had just come *daown*, spoke a language almost unintelli-gible." "Their dress was also peculiar," Robinson added, "and was of the plainest of homespun, cut in such an old-fashioned style that each young girl looked as if she had borrowed her grandmother's gown."

However great such differences may have seemed, most of these young women adjusted. Many of their workmates had been in Lowell only a short while themselves. During the early decades of this era, few women remained in the mills longer than four or five years. Most could remember their own uneasiness and sympathized with the plight of the newcomers. By the mid-1820s, older sisters and cousins had pre-ceded many newcomers, and family networks helped them to overcome whatever fear and loneliness they might have felt.

The women also persevered because of personal resources developed at home. Although the ma-chine-driven pace of work in factories was certainly

7

new, hard work was not. On New England farms of the period, women prepared food, tended gardens, marketed produce, milked cows, and produce butter, cheese, soap, and candles. They were also responsible for making cloth. Homespun was still the most prevalent form of clothing in many rural areas, and farm girls began spinning and weaving at an early age. However baffling the machinery in Lowell cotton mills may have been, the women were all familiar with the basic principles of textile production.

In making the transition from farm to factory, new workers could also count on assistance from their workmates. The company boardinghouses that local corporations had built to house their workers gave women the opportunity to speak to one another about their problems and prospects, their hopes and their fears. Inside the mills, newcomers worked with veterans who taught them the tricks of the trade. They often developed work-sharing arrangements. As Harriet Robinson recalled, workers "stood by one another in the mills; when one wanted to be absent half a day, two or three others would tend an extra loom or frame apiece, so that the absent one might not lose her pay."

As the months passed the women gradually adjusted to factory life. Some even compared their new jobs favorably with work on the farm. But they were never entirely satisfied with their positions. According to one worker, "They would scorn to say they were contented, if asked the question; for it would compromise their Yankee spirit—their pride, penetration, independence, and love of 'freedom and equality' to say they were *contented* with such a life as this." As their experiences grew, mill women developed a strong sense of their own worth and they deeply resented any threat to it.

In Lowell, the first serious challenge to women workers occurred in 1834. Faced with declining

(facing page), A broadside for a "new drama" about the mill girls of Lowell.

WORKING WOMEN AND THE FACTORY SYSTEM

prices and a stagnant market, mill owners imposed a 15 to 20 percent wage cut. An even larger reduction had initially been proposed, but the agents who supervised operations in Lowell had warned the mills' Boston-based directors that the smaller cut would cause trouble enough. Their fears were more than justified. As news of the pay slashes spread, women held meetings to protest the reductions. When one of their leaders was subsequently dismissed, her workmates took their protests into the streets, organizing a mass rally at which they issued a proclamation:

UNION IS POWER

Our present object is to have union and exertion, and we remain in possession of our inalienable rights. We circulate this paper, wishing to obtain the names of all who imbibe the spirit of our patriotic ancestors, who preferred privation to bondage, and parted with all that renders life desirable— and even life itself—to procure independence for their children.

This appeal to revolutionary-era themes received further expression in the poem that ended the proclamation:

> Let oppression shrug her shoulders,
> And a haughty tyrant frown,
> And little upstart Ignorance,
> In mockery look down.
> Yet I value not the feeble threats
> Of Tories in disguise,
> While the flag of Independence
> O'er our noble nation flies.

That striking mill women would invoke the rhetoric of their revolutionary forbearers was not surprising. The meaning of the revolution was still a live issue for this generation of Americans. This was especially so among working people. As the new corporations pushed aside older forms of enterprise, many workers faced uncertain futures. They feared

that the ideals for which their ancestors had struggled were being threatened by "Tory" mill owners who placed return on investment before considerations of justice and equity. It was thus perfectly natural that they would seek to legitimize their own struggles by appealing to the nation's revolutionary past. In so doing, Lowell mill women linked their claims to those of Boston artisans, Lynn shoemakers, and other workers who believed the principles of the Declaration of Independence applied to all Americans.

Such appeals were not enough in 1834. Only one-sixth of the work force joined the strikers, who had chosen an inopportune moment to desert their looms and spinning frames. Most mills had large inventories of finished cloth on hand and were only too happy to curtail operations. But the strike laid the foundation for subsequent actions. Two years later, when the corporations attempted to shift the costs of inflation to workers by raising boarding-house fees, a more broadly based and better-organized walkout forced many mills to rescind the increases. And during the 1840s, Lowell mill women would play a conspicuous role in that decade's shorter-hours movement.

The women who participated in these actions had come a long way from that day when they had stepped down from the baggage wagon and viewed Lowell for the first time. Their conceptions of themselves as both women and workers had broadened considerably. Some even began to envision a new world where class oppression and gender discrimination were things of the past. One such woman was Betsey Chamberlain, who, in an 1841 essay in the *Lowell Offering*, imagined a "Society for the promotion of Industry, Virtue, and Knowledge," which at its annual meeting adopted the following set of resolutions:

9

Sarah Bagley

Sarah Bagley's life began and ended without fanfare. Probably born in New Hampshire, she might have spent her entire life in anonymity had she not joined the thousands of other young women seeking employment in the cotton mills of Massachusetts. By 1836, Bagley was working at Lowell's Hamilton Manufacturing Company. Over the next eleven years, she would become America's first female labor activist.

Evidence suggests that Bagley had no complaints about her first years in the mills. She started a free school for factory women to attend after work. She also wrote about the "Pleasures of Factory Life" in the *Lowell Offering*, a company-controlled magazine known for printing the poems and short stories of the female mill workers. The 1840s, however, were marked by less optimism among the participants in the so-called Lowell Experiment as conditions in the mills worsened.

In the winter of 1844 to 1845, Bagley organized the Lowell Female Labor Reform Association and was chosen vice president. An auxiliary of the New England Workingmen's Association, the LFLRA began with only twelve members but grew to more than five hundred workers by June 1846. The association was concerned with the declining work environment in the mills, including wage cuts, poor sanitary and lighting conditions, and the increasingly common management technique of speeding up machinery without providing additional workers.

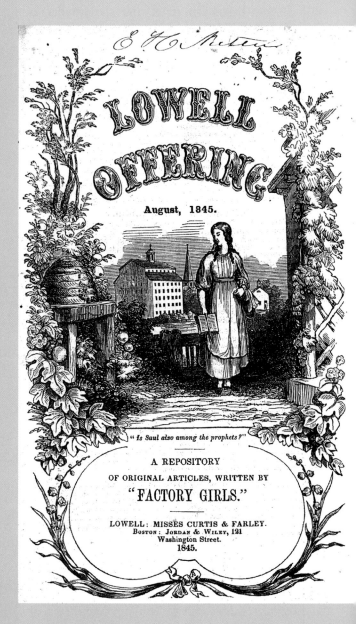

A cover from the *Lowell Offering* that featured the writings of Sarah Bagley and other factory girls from Lowell.

Bagley first tried to express these concerns through submissions to the *Lowell Offering*. When her written observations were rejected by the pro-corporation publication, Bagley took her criticisms of working conditions, and of the *Offering* and its management, to a July 4, 1845, rally in Woburn. Her remarks at that gathering probably led to the disbanding of the *Offering* later that year.

The LFLRA supported the ten-hour day movement of the mid-1840s. Bagley led a vigorous petition drive and submitted thousands of signatures demanding legislation to improve conditions in the mills and for a shorter workday to the Massachusetts House of Representatives. The Committee on Manufacturing conducted hearings, declaring that if petitioners did not come forward, the documents would be dismissed. Bagley and many other workers appeared in Boston to provide dramatic testimony supplementing their signatures, but their appeal was rejected. The committee report acknowledged that there were problems in the mills but put its faith in the corporations to identify the problems and supply the necessary solutions.

By 1847 Bagley had left work in the mills and was employed as a telegraph operator (the first woman in that position in the United States). That same year, she stepped down from the LFLRA and vanished from written history.

1. *Resolved*, That every father of a family who neglects to give his daughters the same advantages for an education as he gives his sons, shall be expelled from this society, and be considered a heathen.

2. *Resolved*, That no member of this society shall exact more than eight hours of labor, out of every twenty-four, of any person in his or her employment.

3. *Resolved*, That, as the laborer is worthy of his hire, the price for labor shall be sufficient to enable the working-people to pay a proper attention to scientific and literary pursuits.

4. *Resolved*, That the wages of females shall be equal to the wages of males, that they may be enabled to maintain proper independence of character, and virtuous deportment.

5. *Resolved*, That no young gentleman of this society shall be allowed to be of age, or to transact business for himself, until he shall have a good knowledge of the English language, understand bookkeeping, both by single and double entry, and be capable of transacting all town business.

6. *Resolved*, That no young lady belonging to this society shall be considered marriageable, who does not understand how to manage the affairs of the kitchen, and who does not, each month, write at least enough to fill one page of octavo.

7. *Resolved*, That we will not patronize the writings of any person who does not spend at least three hours in each day, when health will permit, either in manual labor, or in some employment which will be a public benefit, and which shall not appertain to literary pursuits.

8. *Resolved*, That each member of this society shall spend three hours in each day in the cultivation of the mental faculties, or forfeit membership, extraordinaries excluded.

9. *Resolved*, That industry, virtue and knowledge (not wealth and titles), shall be the standard of respectability for this society.

As Betsey Chamberlain made clear, this was still a dream in 1841. Yet dreams are important, and each generation of Massachusetts working people has had its own vision of the good society.

CHAPTER 2

The Boston Bootmakers in the Supreme Judicial Court

IN THE COLONIAL WORLD OF ARTISANS, NEARLY ALL craftsmen saw themselves as entrepreneurs. Their world was a place where, after achieving proficiency in their trade, artisans could rise from apprentices to journeymen and gradually accumulate the resources needed to become masters and contractors in their own right.

But this world was passing. By the 1820s, most craftsmen would not be able to leave the world of wage earners. As disillusioned journeymen resigned themselves to lives of wage dependency, they became convinced of the need for collective action to protect themselves against poverty and exploitation. And, as such convictions spread and deepened, disputes over wages, hours, and working conditions multiplied.

Journeymen also began to recognize the need for permanent organizations that would better enable them to protect their interests. The first major initia-

An early representation of glass making that appeared in *The People's Magazine*, June 29, 1833.

tive in Boston occurred during the summer of 1830, when local workers formed a workingmen's party that viewed "all attempts to degrade the working classes as so many blows aimed at the destruction of popular virtue—without which no human government can long subsist." Although the party fared poorly in municipal elections and disappeared the following year, workers continued to seek tangible ways to express their solidarity. Many individual trades such as the masons, bakers, and house carpenters created associations of their own, and in March 1834 local artisans representing sixteen crafts and four thousand wage earners organized a citywide union of trades. Six more crafts joined later. At the group's founding convention, leaders issued a Declaration of Rights that asserted "it is the right of workmen, and a duty they owe each other, to associate together."

This was not a right that could be taken for granted. According to ideas about conspiracy that were widespread at the time, journeymen who joined together to further their economic interests represented a threat to society and could be tried as felons.

In a December 1832 charge to a grand jury, Judge Peter Oxenbridge Thacher declared that journeymen's associations both undermined the operation of fundamental economic laws and threatened personal liberties. "All such acts," he told jurors, "infringe upon the freedom of the market, which it is one main object of policy in every well-

The bottoming room in the factory of B. F. Spinney & Co., Lynn, Massachusetts.

regulated state to secure. They violate the freedom of the citizen, which consists not in liberty of person only, but of conduct, and in the right to do as one pleases in all matters not commanded or forbidden by law." Workers who organized in disregard of these maxims could expect little mercy from Thacher. "Whenever individuals array themselves against the law," he concluded, "they should be promptly met, before combination manifests itself in mobs, insurrections, and other civil commotions, which the strong arm of government only can repress."

Boston journeymen bitterly opposed the manner in which the conspiracy doctrine was used to suppress worker organizations. They knew that laws were necessary, but they also believed that, in a democracy, the law should be equally accessible to all citizens. They were troubled by the way in which its growing complexity had made law the special preserve of a privileged elite. The Working Men's party of 1830 gave voice to these fears when it resolved that "people have a right to understand every law made for their government without paying enormous fees for having them expounded by lawyers—by those perhaps who were instrumental in their construction, and in rendering them incomprehensible, even to themselves." The Boston Trades' Union condemned those "Lawyers and Judges [who] lay their heads together, and impose upon us just what laws they please, and execute them as they please, while we tamely submit to grind out the task they assign us with the same patience, and the same spirit and intelligence, too, as a horse in a bark mill."

Among Boston labor leaders of the period, no one challenged the conservative vision of social order more articulately or more defiantly than Seth Luther. A journeyman carpenter from Rhode Island, Luther played a prominent role in forming the Boston Trades' Union of the mid-thirties. Despite limited formal schooling, he was also an accomplished orator. "Men of property," he remarked in an 1832 address, "find no fault with combinations to extinguish fires and to protect their *precious persons* from danger. But if *poor men* ask JUSTICE, it is a most HORRIBLE COMBINATION." This was nothing new, Luther added. Patriots of an earlier era had faced similar obstacles: "The Declaration of Independence was the work of a combination, and was as hateful to the TRAITORS and TORIES of those days, as combinations among working men are now to the *avaricious* MONOPOLIST and *purse-proud* ARISTOCRAT."

This was not the only occasion on which Luther employed revolutionary-era themes to make a point. His father had fought in that conflict, and Luther spent much of his life seeking to spread the principles that had prompted such sacrifices. It was fitting that his fullest statement on the conspiracy doctrine came four years later in a Fourth of July address. There had recently been five conspiracy prosecutions against New York and Philadelphia journeymen. He focused his attack on Judge Ogden Edwards, who, in presiding over the best known of these cases, had asserted that "self-constituted societies will not be permitted to rear their crests in this country." "If you can find anything more tyrannical than this in all the history of despotic power," Luther declared, "I should like to see it." Aristocratic beliefs of this sort had no place in a democratic society and should not go unchallenged: "We can, and do, tell the learned judge that 'self-constituted societies' *do* exist, *must* exist, and *shall* exist, even if we have

to defend ourselves with the bayonet's burnished point."

Although violence did not erupt in Massachusetts, Boston became the site of the period's most celebrated conspiracy trial, *Commonwealth v. Hunt*. It centered on Jeremiah Horne, a member of the Boston Society of Journeymen Bootmakers, who in 1840 refused to pay a fine for violating the group's rules. When the union later persuaded Horne's employer to discharge him, he retained a lawyer to bring charges of criminal conspiracy against the society.

In the trial that followed, the Bootmakers were defended by Robert Rantoul, Jr., a prominent Democratic politician and social reformer. Rantoul argued that, because association itself was no crime, the prosecution had to demonstrate that the society had committed an unlawful or injurious act. Yet, as Horne's employer testified, he had willingly complied with the Bootmakers' request. It was a sound defense, but the judge hearing the case was none other than Peter Oxenbridge Thacher. In his instructions to the jury, Thacher stated that the Bootmakers' Society represented "a new power in the state, unknown to its constitution and laws, and subversive of their equal spirit." Were such combinations allowed to operate freely, he added, "all industry and enterprise would be suspended, and all property would become insecure." Thacher's prodding was apparently effective, for the jury brought back a guilty verdict.

Robert Rantoul filed a bill of exceptions to Thacher's jury instructions, which he subsequently argued before the Massachusetts Supreme Judicial Court. There the case was heard by Lemuel Shaw, one of the era's most eminent jurists. During his more than three decades as chief justice of the state's highest tribunal, Shaw had a greater influence on the

Lemuel Shaw (1781-1861) by Southworth and Hawes. Shaw, Chief Justice
of the Massachusetts Supreme Judicial Court, handed down the first decision
that said unions had the legal right to exist.

An Experiment in Industrial Utopia

For four and a half years from 1842 to 1846 a radical communitarian experiment called the Northampton Association of Education and Industry pursued an ideal of economic cooperation and social harmony. Founded on principles of racial equality, women's rights, and religious toleration, the Association sought to reform the emerging industrial system from competition to cooperation in a community that combined work, domestic life, and education.

Property was not owned communally. Rather, the founders formed a joint stock company with holdings that included farmland, houses, and a silk factory on a river at the edge of Northampton. Like Brook Farm and other contemporary experiments, the Northampton Association drew membership from social reformers of the day. It grew quite large in scale for the time, with as many as one hundred twenty members in residence, many living on the converted second floor of the factory which also housed the communal dining hall.

Combining agriculture and silk manufacture with cooperative ownership and communal social arrangements, the community challenged many cultural assumptions of the nineteenth century. Founded by abolitionists and dedicated to racial equality, the community accepted black men and women as equals, one of the few institutions in the United States to do so at the time. Among the free and fugitive slaves in residence was the abolitionist leader Sojourner Truth.

With membership privileges equal to men's, women participated fully in the meetings and votes that shaped the policies of the community. Domestic labor was accorded equal value with other work, but the larger debate concerned the morality of capitalism in general. Founders who had anticipated the community would function under a wage system withdrew when the general membership pushed the community in a more radical direction, renouncing the wage system altogether and replacing it with a system of subsistence allowances and profit-sharing. The membership also voted a reduction of the workday from the usual twelve hours to eleven and eventually to ten hours. Bonds of fellowship with reformers elsewhere were strong. Correspondence with labor leader Sarah Bagley even proposed a partnership of the community with the women millworkers in Lowell.

Education of the community's many children was progressive, engaging girls as well as boys in vigorous physical exercise. For a time the community attracted boarding students from nonmember families wanting their children to partake of an education that combined work and study.

For many members, participation was an expression of deeply held religious belief. The community itself, however, was nonsectarian. The staunch moral convictions of its members played a part in the community's making poor business decisions that led to mounting debt and eventual dissolution.

The treasurer Samuel Hill abided through the years of experimentation, during which the community enrolled a total of some 240 members. Hill gradually assumed the association's debt personally and went on to oversee the

transformation of the community into a factory village. Naming the settlement Florence, after Italy's center of silk manufacturing, Hill and others who remained continued to seek an ideal of social harmony in neighborhood life. Business decisions would be strictly separate, however. Economic cooperation now consisted of business partnerships and interlocking directorates among the owners of the factories that sprang up in the community's wake. Hill's concern for social improvement began to be expressed in philanthropy. But, as an immigrant work force arrived, the workday in Hill's factories returned to twelve hours.

An 1864 photograph of the abolitionist Sojourner Truth who earlier had spent time with the Northampton Association of Education and Industry.

development of American law than most U.S. Supreme Court members of the time. His decisions were widely read and highly influential. On the bench, Shaw was an imposing figure who severely chastised the slightest breach of courtroom etiquette.

The Bootmakers were apprehensive about Shaw's decision, as it was common knowledge that he was no friend of labor. A decade earlier, he had warned of the threat that associations, "animated by a strong sense of common feeling and interest," posed to the operation of the law. And in the same year that he ruled on *Hunt*, another of his decisions established that employers were not liable for injuries sustained by workers in workplace accidents where it could be shown that another employee's actions contributed to the mishap. Following Shaw's lead, other courts broadly interpreted the principle in ways that relieved employers of a major responsibility and sharply limited efforts to obtain compensation for work-related injuries.

Yet Shaw ruled in favor of the Bootmakers' Society. Thacher had plainly acted in a heavy-handed manner, and Shaw doubtless recognized that such actions undermine popular regard for the law itself. His decision not only upheld workers' right to organize, it also stated that workers had a right to withhold their labor to achieve such ends, so long as they did so in a peaceable manner and without violating existing contracts.

Shaw based his decision on a belief that associations—among businesspeople as well as workers—were inevitable in a market society. That being the case, the law's main function was to determine whether a given combination had been organized for "useful and honorable purposes" or "dangerous and pernicious ones." Shaw further felt that competition between capital and labor benefited society just as much as competition among business did. By ruling as he did, he suggested that competition belonged in the workplace rather than the courts.

Commonwealth v. Hunt was a landmark decision for workers in Massachusetts and across the country. Where earlier conspiracy cases had left the impression that unions were unlawful institutions, Shaw's ruling explicitly acknowledged their legality. Its approval of union actions to obtain closed shops was a clear advance for workers. *Hunt*, however, did not signal the end of conspiracy prosecutions. They flourished again during the closing decades of the nineteenth century, before fading into disuse as employers turned increasingly to labor injunctions that barred a broad range of union activities. Throughout, workers could expect little assistance from the courts. As Seth Luther said in an 1836 address condemning conspiracy trials: "The very fact that societies formed by Mechanics and Workingmen are attacked with such venomous malignity, by the leaders of the aristocracy, ought to convince us that in union alone there is safety." This indeed was a very early lesson in solidarity.

CHAPTER 3

The Movement for the Ten-Hour Day

A s shops grew larger and business competi-
tion intensified in the early nineteenth century across New England, the work process continued to change rapidly. The growing use of machinery began the process of the de-skilling of artisan work that would continue into the next century. The informal workplaces of an earlier era were being replaced by a more rigorous daily regimen where workers were losing control of the work process.

In these changing workplaces, workers often found themselves toiling much harder, with less control, and for significantly less pay. An 1834 article in the *New England Artisan* suggested that workers "keep up wages by the only effectual plan that can

A drawing from *Leslie's Illustrated Weekly* dated June 29, 1872, depicting one of many marches in favor of shorter working hours.

be devised, viz.: the reduction from time to time, of the hours of labor, nicely proportioned to the excess of supply over the demand of the products of labor." Then and only then would "labor saving machinery be a blessing, and not a curse."

In mills such as those in Lowell, the hours were oppressive. The old habit of working from sun-up to sun-down became intensified as employers and machinery demanded a constant pace. During the late 1830s, mounting competition in a contracting market caused a steady decline in cloth prices. As profits sagged, mill agents sought to cut costs by intensifying the work pace through the adoption of such practices as the stretchout and speedup— increasing the number of machines a worker was responsible for and running the machines at higher speeds. As their workloads grew, workers found the industry's thirteen- and fourteen-hour workdays unbearable. "The time we are required to labor is altogether too long," one worker declared. "If anyone doubts it, let them come into our mills of a summer's day, at four or five o'clock, in the afternoon, and see the drooping, weary persons moving about, as though their legs were hardly able to support their bodies."

As the campaign for a shorter workday progressed, it became closely linked to the growing problem of child labor. Although children had always worked in New England, they had traditionally done so within family settings that provided for their moral and intellectual development. This responsibility extended to masters who took on apprentices, as well as parents who supervised their children's labor on regional farms. By the 1830s, however, most masters had long ceased paying much attention to such duties.

Equally troubling was the large number of chil-

dren in the early industrial work force. These were mostly children in their teen years, but also included some children as young as eight or nine years old. Indeed, the latter problem had become so serious that in 1832 the New England Association of Farmers, Mechanics, and Other Working Men appointed a committee to investigate the matter. It found that in most textile mills children were required to work thirteen to fourteen hours a day. The committee added that these youths "are generally the offspring of parents whose poverty has made them entirely dependent on the will of their employers, and are very seldom taken from the mills and placed in school." To correct this deplorable situation, the association urged members to petition state legislatures for a ten-hour day and "some wholesome regulations in regard to the education of children" employed in factories. As Horace Mann of Massachusetts, the founder of the public school movement, described: "It was the tradesmen who first came to the legislature to plead the cause of public education because they realized that their sons and daughters would forever remain slaves to an industrial machine unless given an equal opportunity for education with the sons and daughters of the wealthy."

But the concerns of the association were broader than just the working conditions of child workers. These children would someday be voters, and if they were to fulfill their responsibilities as citizens they needed what the committee called "an education suitable to the character of American freemen." Without such preparation, they would be ill equipped to maintain their independence in the face of upper-class manipulation—a situation that could only end in "the final prostration of their liberties at the shrine of a powerful aristocracy." It was no sur-

An illustration from *Harper's Weekly* (1861) depicting work in an early
firearms factory similar to the well-known facility in Springfield.

The Voice of Industry, the newspaper of the New England Workingmen's Association, one of the organizations fighting for shorter working hours.

prise that Boston trade unionists made citizenship rights a central part of their campaign for shorter hours.

The famous "Ten-Hour Circular" of 1835, written by Seth Luther and two other local journeymen, condemned the "tyrannical system which compels the operative Mechanic to exhaust his physical and mental powers by excessive toil, until he has no desire but to eat and sleep, and in many cases he has no power to do either from extreme debility." It also

declared: "We have rights, and we have duties to perform as American Citizens and members of society, which forbid us to dispose of more than Ten Hours for a day's work." Employers would do well to acknowledge these rights, the circular added, for they had been established "by the blood of our fathers, shed on our battlefields in the War of the Revolution, . . . and no earthly power shall resist our righteous claims with impunity."

The depression of 1837 dealt a crushing blow to trade unions throughout the Northeast, but it was not long before workers were again organizing to shorten the workday. The impetus came from Fall River mechanics. In 1842, they included a demand for a ten-hour workday in a petition to the Massachusetts legislature. Two years later, they called for a region-wide convention on the question. Held in October 1844 in Boston, the gathering resulted in the formation of the New England Workingmen's Association (NEWA). Like their counterparts a decade earlier, labor leaders of the 1840s continued to stress the connection between ten hours and citizenship. Association meetings rarely concluded without resolving that "an abridgment of the hours of labor" was absolutely essential to "render every citizen of the commonwealth worthy and capable to perform the sacred duties of a freeman."

These two efforts to achieve a ten-hour day differed in important ways. Middle-class reformers played an important role in the NEWA, whose activities went beyond the ten-hour day to include other issues such as land reform. Even more significant was the active role played by women. Where Seth Luther and his colleagues excluded women from their public activities, the NEWA constitution extended "all the rights, privileges and obligations" of the association to women's labor groups. The contributions of women workers from the Lowell

Charles Dale Turnball, an early Boston craftsman.

mills were particularly important. In 1843 and 1844, they sent ten-hour-day petitions to the legislature, each of which contained more than a thousand signatures. In December 1844, they formed their own independent organization, the Lowell Female Labor Reform Association (LFLRA).

Although they could not vote, mill women also employed the citizenship theme in their campaign for shorter hours. They did so by pointing to their role as mothers. To prepare children for the duties and responsibilities of citizenship, they contended, women had to be at least as well informed as men because "the mother educates the man." Conditions in the New England mills prevented women from obtaining the education needed to perform this vital task. As Sarah Bagley, the first leader of the Lowell Association, put it: "At one time, they tell us that our 'free institutions' are based upon the *virtue* and *intelligence* of the American people, and the influence of the mother form and mould the man—and the next breath, that the way to make the mothers of the next generation virtuous, is to inclose them within the brick walls of a cotton mill from twelve and a half to thirteen and a half hours per day."

To some degree, this argument supported the belief that it was a man's world and that women's place was in the home, where as mothers they would carry out the child rearing. But there is also evidence that some mill women were moving beyond the strict separation of activities between men and women. In an 1846 letter to the *Voice of Industry*, one female worker noted how unfair it was that society offered women no means of developing their abilities outside marriage. "It may be," she wrote, "that most women are so dwarfed and weakened, that they believe that dressing, cooking, and loving" represent all that one could reasonably expect from life; "but Nature still asserts her rights, and there will always

Ten-Hour Circular

First published in *The Man* on May 13, 1835, this was Seth Luther's "call to arms" for the ten-hour-day movement:

We have been too long subjected to the odious, cruel, unjust, and tyrannical system which compels the operative Mechanic to exhaust his physical and mental powers by excessive toil, until he has no desire but to eat and sleep, and in many cases he has no power to do either from extreme debility.

We contend that no man or body of men have a right to require of us that we should toil as we have hitherto done under the old system of labor.

We go further. No man or body of men who require such excessive labor can be friends to the country or the Rights of Man. We also say, that we have rights and we have duties to perform as American Citizens and members of society, which forbid us to dispose of more than Ten Hours for a day's work.

We cannot, we will not, longer be mere slaves to inhuman, insatiable and unpitying avarice. We have taken a firm and decided stand, to obtain the acknowledgment of those rights to enable us to perform those duties to God, our Country and ourselves. . . .

We assert and challenge the world to controvert the position that excessive labor has been the immediate cause of more intemperance than all other causes combined. Physical exhaustion craves and will have excitement of some kind, and the cause of Temperance never will prevail until slavery among Mechanics shall cease from the land.

We are friends to temperance "in all things," but any man who requires of us excessive labor is intemperate; if he is not actuated by ardent spirits, he is controlled by a spirit of inhumanity equally fatal to human happiness. . . .

The property holders in this city are dependent night and day upon the Mechanics, to man their Fire Engines; good policy might seem to dictate to them the expediency of providing a new set of firemen, before they starve the present ones or drive them to the extremity of leaving their Engine Houses desolate unto them. We are willing to bear our portion of the burthens, and perform our part of the services of social life, if we can be treated as men and not as beasts of burthen. We claim by the blood of our fathers, shed on our battle-fields in the War of the Revolution, the rights of American Freemen, and no earthly power shall resist our righteous claims with impunity. . . .

Mechanics of Boston—stand firm—Be true to yourselves. Now is the time to enroll your names on the scroll of history as the undaunted enemies of oppression, as the enemies of mental, moral and physical degradation, as the friends of the human race.

be those too strong to be satisfied, with a dress, a pudding, or a beau, though they may take each in its turn, as a portion of life." Sarah Bagley understood this when she told the first regular meeting of the New England Workingmen's Association: "For the last half century it has been deemed a violation of women's sphere to appear before the public as a speaker; but when our rights are trampled upon and

we appeal in vain to legislators, what shall we do but appeal to the people?"

Participation in the ten-hour crusade allowed working women to escape the narrow family and work roles to which they had been relegated and to enter the world of politics and public debate. The best example was the 1845 petition campaign, which was spearheaded by the Lowell Female Reform Asso-

Song of the Ten Hour Workingman

"Song of the Ten Hour Workingman," which first appeared in *The Mechanic* on May 4, 1844, was one of several songs adapted for the ten-hour campaign. It was sung to the tune of "Auld Lang Syne."

I am a Ten hour workingman!
   I glory in the name;
Though now by "all day" minions hissed,
   And covered o'er with shame;
It is a spell of light and power—
   The watchword of the free:—
Who spurns it in his trial-hour,
   A craven soul is he.

I am a Ten hour workingman!
   Then urge me not to pause:
For joyfully do I enlist
   In FREEDOM's sacred cause:
A nobler strife the world ne'er saw,
   Th'enslaved to disenthral;
I am a soldier for the war,
   Whatever may befall!

I am a Ten hour workingman,
   Oppression's deadly foe;
In God's great strength will I resist,
   And lay the monster low;
In God's great name do I demand,
   To all be freedom given,
That peace and joy may fill the land,
   And songs go up to heaven.

I am a Ten hour workingman!
   No threats shall awe my soul,
No perils cause me to desist,
   No bribes my acts control;
A freeman will I live and die,
   In sunshine and in shade,
And raise my voice for liberty,
   Of naught on earth afraid.

ciation. When the Massachusetts House of Representatives Committee on Manufacturing attempted to kill the women's initiative by requiring association members to give public testimony on the question, the women protested. But the committee, following the lead of its chairman, William Schouler, proprietor of the *Lowell Courier*, issued a report dismissing the petition. The women condemned the report and singled out Schouler, whom they characterized as a "corporation machine, or tool," for political retribution, declaring that they would use their "best endeavors and influence to keep him in the 'city of spindles,' where he belongs, and not trouble Boston folks with him." As a result of their efforts, Schouler

lost his bid for another term in office. Association members thanked Lowell voters "for consigning [him] to the obscurity he so justly deserves."

Lawmakers did not enact the ten-hour law women millworkers demanded. Workers would wait another three decades before the Massachusetts legislature passed such a measure. But the ten-hour crusade was not in vain. The legislative effort failed, but many Bay State manufacturers shifted from a thirteen- to an eleven-hour workday in order to deflect further criticism. And beyond its leadership in promoting progressive labor legislation, the Lowell Female Reform Association helped create a new civic role for Massachusetts women.

PART II

FROM SLAVERY TO FREEDOM, 1850-1865

On May 9, 1848, trade unionists met in Faneuil Hall to honor the European revolutions of that year and to rejoice over the freedoms growing at home and abroad. But the assembly went out of its way to condemn "the despotic attitude of Slave Power" in the South. "The question of slavery is in truth a question of labor," declared the *Voice of Industry*. No social question could be addressed without confronting slavery, said the *New Era*, a Boston workingman's paper: "It cannot be avoided. It must be extinguished."

Massachusetts was the birthplace of the abolitionist movement. Beginning with the publication of William Lloyd Garrison's *Liberator* and David Walker's *Appeal*, slaves began to look north to the Bay State as a beacon of freedom. Frederick Douglass, a Maryland slave, escaped to the Commonwealth, where he sought his freedom. Arriving in New Bedford, he was awestruck with the social diversity of the community and the liberties afforded to free blacks. Massachusetts had made strides toward racial equality inconceivable to a black man born into slavery.

Yet the dream of a just and equal society—the same dream that the Reverend Martin Luther King would express one hundred years later—was sorely incomplete. On the docks in New Bedford, Douglass quickly learned that he would be unable to practice his trade. Despite the widespread support of Bay Staters for the abolition of slavery, free black laborers in Massachusetts suffered severely from the racial discrimination practiced by white employers and workers alike. Both the freedom Douglass enjoyed and the barriers he faced helped shape the man Douglass would later become.

As the antislavery movement gained momentum in Massachusetts, the daughters and sons of white freemen began to complain bitterly that their own freedom had been sacrificed to the new capitalist wage and profit system. In the great shoe strike of 1860—the largest in U.S. history until that time—women shoe stitchers in Lynn marched under a banner that read "American Ladies Will Not be Slaves."

To win the support of northern mechanics and factory workers, Abraham Lincoln campaigned as an apostle of free labor, praising the virtues of the producers and condemning the excesses of the profiteers. In 1859, Lincoln declared "that labor is prior to, and independent of capital; that, in fact, capital is the fruit of labor, and could never have existed if labor had not first existed; that labor can exist without capital, but that capital could never have existed without labor. Hence . . . labor is . . . greatly the superior of capital."

Massachusetts workers not only fought to extend free labor to the South, they applied President Lincoln's values to their own condition. When the Civil War ended in 1865, they held the Commonwealth to the standards their martyred president had so eloquently articulated. On November 2, 1865, two years after he founded the Boston Eight Hour League, Ira Steward addressed an overflow crowd of workingmen at Faneuil Hall. He read a list of resolutions, concluding that "we rejoice that the rebel aristocracy of the South has been crushed . . . that beneath the glorious shadow of our flag men of every clime, lineage and color are free. But . . . we yet want it to be known that the workingmen of America will in future claim a more equal share in the wealth their industry creates . . . and a more equal participation in . . . those free institutions . . . defended on many a bloody field of battle."

In the 1850s and 1860s, the labor movement was changing. Gone was the "community of interest" between the employer and the employed that had once existed. In its place, a more aggressive and ambitious labor movement was emerging. No longer content to form mere "benefit" associations, workers struck, marched, and became active in politics in communities across the Commonwealth and the nation. And while they clung to their revolutionary heritage, they also began to look ahead to new solutions and new tactics. And while divisions among them—between black and white, men and women, Catholic and Protestant—would persist, working people were learning important lessons in solidarity.

CHAPTER 4

Frederick Douglass and the Antislavery Movement in Massachusetts

O N A SEPTEMBER DAY IN 1838, A YOUNG BLACK man and his wife stepped down from a stagecoach in front of the main hotel in New Bedford. He was called Frederick Johnson—at least that was the name he had given several days earlier upon his marriage in New York City. Before that he had been Frederick Bailey, a Maryland slave. Soon he would take yet another name, one by which he would be

The drawing of Frederick Douglass that appeared in the first edition of his *Narrative of the Life of Frederick Douglass, an American Slave*, published in Boston in 1845.

known for the rest of his life. At his death forty-seven years later, Frederick Douglass would be the most famous African American of his time.

But for the moment Douglass worried about establishing a home for himself and his new wife. At the time of his arrival, New Bedford was a thriving community of more than twelve thousand people. Walking along the wharves, he noticed that everything was "managed with a much more scrupulous regard to economy, both of men and things, time and strength, than in the country from which I had come. I found that even the laboring classes lived in better houses, that their houses were more elegantly furnished and were more abundantly supplied with conveniences and comforts, than the houses of many who owned slaves on the Eastern Shore of Maryland."

In addition to this prosperity, a fugitive slave such as Douglass found New Bedford appealing because of its racial tolerance. This stemmed in part from the prominent role of Quakers in town affairs. The Society of Friends had long opposed slavery, and local families such as the Rotches, Rodmans, and Grinnels staunchly upheld that commitment. But tolerance was also a matter of necessity. During the heyday of the whaling industry, New Bedford contained one of the most culturally diverse communities in America. Local ships that traversed the globe in search of whales often returned with mariners from as far away as Asia, Africa, and Polynesia. Given such a diverse work force and the work that needed

A Quote from Frederick Douglass

If there is no struggle there is no progress. Those who profess to favor freedom and yet depreciate agitation . . . want crops without plowing up the ground. They want rain, without thunder and lightening. They want the ocean without the awful roar of its many waters. This struggle may be a moral one; it may be a physical one; or it may be both moral and physical; but it must be a struggle. Power concedes nothing without a demand. It never did and it never will.

—From a conference in Canadaigua, New York, 1857

to be done, New Bedford was considerably more accepting of others than many Massachusetts cities and towns.

During the late 1830s, the black community in New Bedford numbered more than a thousand people. It included runaway slaves, who had begun arriving as early as 1819, and freeborn descendants of Africans, who had been enslaved and brought to New England generations earlier. It also included black seamen from the Cape Verde Islands and recently emancipated immigrants from the West Indies. Massachusetts was one of only five states in which blacks could then vote.

Having just left a region where teaching slaves to read or write was a criminal offense, Douglass was amazed that New Bedford, like most other Bay State communities outside Boston, enrolled African American children in its public schools on a nondis-criminatory basis. It was, he later wrote, "the nearest approach to freedom and equality that I had ever seen. I could have landed in no part of the United States where I should have found a more striking and gratifying contrast, not only to life generally in the South, but in the condition of the colored people there, than in New Bedford."

Douglass's hopes for a different society, however, were soon dashed. The civic freedoms afforded to the black community did not extend to the workplace. He had been trained as a ship caulker, and one of the main reasons he came to New Bedford was that a New York acquaintance assured him he would have little trouble finding suitable employment there. But after being hired to help caulk a vessel being outfitted for a whaling voyage, Douglass reported being told by prospective workmates "that every white man would leave the ship in her unfinished condition if I struck a blow at my trade upon her."

This was a serious setback. Caulking was skilled labor and paid two dollars a day, a princely wage that would have enabled Douglass to begin saving money to purchase one of those "neat, modest, and convenient" houses that dotted the hills of New Bedford. If he were forced to work as a common laborer, earning at best half that much, his trajectory would change dramatically. Although he soon left New Bedford, he never forgot what his life would have been had he remained in the Bay State whaling community that was his first home as a freeman. In the final edition of his autobiography, he wrote: "The last forty years of my life might have been spent on the wharves of New Bedford, rolling oil casks, loading ships for whaling voyages, sawing wood, putting in coal, picking up a job here and there, wherever I could find one, and in the race for life and bread, holding my own with difficulty against gauntsided poverty."

While working on the New Bedford docks with free black men, Douglass wrote later, he became "imbued with the spirit of liberty." After hearing a speech in Mechanics Hall by the Boston abolitionist William Lloyd Garrison, the runaway slave decided to dedicate his life to freeing his brothers and sisters who remained in bondage.

As tensions between the North and South escalated, Frederick Douglass achieved national prominence as an abolitionist. He returned to New Bedford in 1856 to address an antislavery meeting. Commenting on the speech he gave that evening, the white abolitionist Samuel Rodman observed: "The years that have elapsed since I last heard him

The ship *Savoia* arriving in New Bedford with Cape Verdean immigrants.

The crew of the *John R. Manta* whaleboat at the oars. The sail and mast are stowed down the center of the boat, while the harpoons in the front are ready for action.

have improved his oratory, the power of which is indicated by the fact that the most quiet and respectful attention was given through his address, which did not end till half past ten o'clock." Even more impressive, Rodman added, was the newly won respect that Douglass and other black activists now commanded: "The scene was in strange contrast with that in our town about twenty years ago when the New England Abolition Society was mobbed and their meeting broken up, though white men of character and talent were the speakers. Here was a meeting called by colored men, who alone occupied the platform, with a gratified audience of about a thousand people, a majority of whom were white and more than half women."

Many Massachusetts working people enlisted in the abolitionist crusade as part of a great freedom struggle. Thomas Wentworth Higginson, an eloquent antislavery activist, went so far as to say that in Massachusetts abolitionism was "predominantly a people's movement . . . far stronger for a time in factories and shoe shops than in pulpits and colleges." Abolitionism was especially strong among shoemakers because, as Higginson noted, "radicalism went with the smell of leather." Not all workers favored abolition, however, and even those who did rarely welcomed the arrival of free blacks in their workplaces and neighborhoods.

Frederick Douglass became an ardent critic of the discrimination free black workers faced in the North at the hands of white workers. He also bemoaned the displacement of free black labor by desperate immigrants. Discouraged about the exclusion of blacks from white organizations, Douglass helped organize the American League of Colored Laborers in 1850 to foster training in agriculture and industrial arts and to encourage laborers to start their own businesses.

At the time of Douglass's arrival, New Bedford

was the nation's foremost whaling center and was growing rapidly. Between 1837 and 1845, the number of local ships employed in the whale fishery increased from 169 to 242 vessels. The amount of whalebone used by manufacturers for garment stays and umbrella ribs rose nearly tenfold from 305,170 to 2,532,445 pounds. The combined take in sperm oil and whale oil quintupled from 2,472,735 to 12,651,591 gallons, whale oil still being the most commonly used illuminant. And as oil prices soared

throughout the 1840s, New Bedford prospered. Within Massachusetts, only textiles and shoes stood ahead of whaling and the manufacture of whaling products as the state's leading industries.

At the foundation of this prosperity were the courageous, hard-bitten whalers who sailed down the Acushnet River each year to hunt whales in the far corners of the globe. Although Frederick Douglass never enlisted for a whaling voyage, many other African Americans did. More than three

Coopers (barrel makers) tipping a full cask of whale oil at Merrill's Wharf, New Bedford.

thousand African Americans signed up for New Bedford whaling expeditions between 1800 and 1860. Despite the rigid discipline and other hardships of life at sea, shipping out had certain attractions for black workers. As a rule, they received pay equal to that of whites in comparable positions. They were also less likely than African Americans in land-bound industries to encounter discrimination on the job. Given the perils of sea life, whalers were much more concerned about a workmate's competence than his race.

That African Americans had achieved some prominence in the industry made whaling even more attractive to black job seekers. During the first half of the nineteenth century, black mariners served as mates and boat-steerers on numerous whaling ships. Although merchant vessels rarely set sail with a black captain at the helm, African Americans commanded a number of whaling vessels. This was especially so in New Bedford, where the black merchant and sea captain Paul Cuffe (1759–1817) had established a family-based shipping business that organized whaling voyages as late as the 1840s.

Once at sea, blacks shared the same dangers and hardships that confronted all nineteenth-century whalers. James Henry Gooding, a black mariner who shipped out on several New Bedford whaling voyages, penned the following lines in memory of Eli Dodge, a shipmate who died in one such incident.

> He ofttimes with us did the monster pursue,
> The huge monster king of the deep,
> But now he is gone and his journey is through,
> Where loud billows roll he does sleep.
>
> How little we thought, but a moment before,
> When near us he bravely did contend,
> With the huge monster then weltering in its gore,
> That he would to hades Eli send.

The bark *Helen Mar* in New Bedford, Massachusetts.

By the 1850s, when Gooding wrote this and other poems of whaling life, he was one of a diminishing number of black sailors. As the discrimination that had long characterized many land-based industries spread seaward, African Americans were increasingly confined to galley work. This was particularly devastating for black whalers, who received a "lay," or a proportion of a voyage's catch, rather than a fixed wage. Workers who could expect no more than a cook's 1/150th share had little chance of ever making a decent living. After returning from a forty-five-month whaling expedition on the *Sunbeam*, where he served as a cook, James Gooding was paid $114.42 — approximately $2.50 a month — and that was better than most people in comparable positions made.

Later, when southern secession gave way to civil war during the spring of 1861, New Bedford African Americans immediately issued a set of resolutions proclaiming their readiness to fight. Several years later, when the U.S. government finally began accepting such offers, the city's young black men rushed to the colors. One of the first to enlist was the former whaleman James Henry Gooding. Having braved the perils of an Arctic whaling expedition, Gooding was well prepared for the hazards of combat. His reports from camp, which appeared regularly in the *New Bedford Mercury*, indicated that his local comrades in the famous Fifty-fourth Massachusetts were equally ready: "They are all anxious to perfect themselves in drill that they may the sooner meet the Rebs, and they all feel determined to fight; they all say this is their wish, and I cannot doubt it, for there seems to be a sort of preternatural earnestness about their expressions which no one can mistake."

But the discrimination that had plagued so many African Americans in civilian life followed them into the military. Where white recruits were paid thirteen dollars a month, their black counterparts received only ten. Apart from considerations of basic justice, this issue created an experiential bond among nearly all African Americans—from eminent public figures such as Frederick Douglass to struggling mariners such as James Henry Gooding. As Douglass worked behind the scenes in Washington to equalize the pay of black and white soldiers, the former whaleman emerged as a powerful voice from the ranks. For Gooding, as he made clear in a letter to President Lincoln, equal pay was a matter of personal dignity as well as economic need: "The Regt. do pray that they be assured their service will be fairly appreciated by paying them as American *Soldiers*, not as menial hirelings. Black men, you may well know, are poor; three dollars per month will supply their needy Wives and little ones with fuel."

Although African Americans would win the fight for equal pay in the military, the fight was only one of many such struggles that would consume their energies in the years ahead. Frederick Douglass would continue to play a part in these campaigns; sadly, James Henry Gooding would not. He died in the Andersonville, Georgia, prison camp in July 1864. He was only twenty-six years old at the time, and his maturing eloquence and expanding vision of black rights never reached full fruition. We can only guess what role he might have played in later battles for racial justice. Yet we do know this: like Douglass, Gooding knew that true democracy would never flourish without equality.

CHAPTER 5

"Free Labor" Triumphs in the Civil War

A NEW AGGRESSIVENESS APPEARED IN THE MASSA-chusetts labor movement in the late 1840s and 1850s. It was reflected in the spread of strikes and culminated in one of the greatest workers' protests in the history of the nation. The massive shoe strike began on the morning of February 22, 1860, when local shoemakers marched through the streets of Lynn to employers' shops and handed in their working tools.

The previous three years had been a dismal time in New England shoe towns. The increasing use of technology pushed production in the shoe industry far ahead of demand. The depression of 1857 only intensified competition. As prices plummeted, manufacturers sought to weather the crisis by slashing wages—to as little as fifty cents a day at some Lynn shops. Many hard-pressed shoemakers could not pay off debts incurred during the winter layoff.

The shoemakers (or cordwainers, as they were then called) who made Lynn the nation's shoe city enjoyed a long history of democratic thought and independent behavior. They began meeting in 1858, and by the winter of 1860 demanded that shoe manufacturers adopt a standardized wage schedule. When the employers refused, the workers began the largest strike witnessed by that generation of Americans. Before it was over, twenty thousand shoemakers deserted their workplaces and another twenty thousand people participated in various meetings and parades organized by the strikers.

They chose to begin the walkout on Washington's Birthday to identify themselves as bearers of an equal-rights tradition rooted in the first American Revolution. This was clear in the "Cordwainers' Song," a strike anthem composed by Lynn poet and historian Alonzo Lewis:

> Shoemakers of Lynn, be brave!
> Renew your resolves again;
> Sink not to the state of slave,
> But stand for your rights like men!
>
> Resolve by your native soil,
> Resolve by your fathers' graves,
> You will live by your honest toil,
> But never consent to be slaves!
>
> The workman is worthy of his hire,
> No tyrant shall hold us in thrall;
> They may order their soldiers to fire,
> But we'll stick to the hammer and awl.
>
> Better days will restore us our rights,
> The future shall shine o'er the past;
> We shall triumph by justice and right,
> For like men we'll hold onto the last!

Though unrecognized in the "Cordwainers' Song," women played a pivotal role in this struggle in Lynn. Indeed, women occupied a central position in developments transforming the shoe industry. In the production system that took shape during the first half of the nineteenth century, entrepreneurs shipped cut stock to shoemakers who, working by

This drawing from *Leslie's Illustrated Weekly*, March 17, 1860, depicts the strike by women shoemakers at Lynn.

leading employers centralized production in major manufacturing centers such as Lynn and further mechanized the production process.

In 1852, manufacturers adapted Singer sewing machines to stitch the light leather used in the upper parts of shoes, thereby reducing the need for home-based binders. In the process, the shoe bosses created what one contemporary observer called "a new and more expansive class of 'machine girls' whose capacity for labor was only limited by the capabilities of the machines over which they presided."

Working outside the shelter of their parents' households, where they had controlled the pace of their own work, the factory-based "machine girls" labored ten or more hours a day at hand-cranked or foot-powered sewing machines. Martha Osbourne Barrett, a Salem shop stitcher, wrote numerous entries in her diary that read simply: "A day of toil, hard physical labor" and "Have been to the shop and am weary." As another worker wrote to the *New England Mechanic* in 1859, advocating a reduction of hours: "Few persons except those blessed with unusual vigor of constitution can pursue this employment steadily ten hours a day, for any considerable period, without finding themselves injuriously affected."

Workers using traditional hand methods could not keep up with the new machines, whose productivity increased as manufacturers made improvements on early models. In the 1850s, shoe manufacturers, starved for "hands," started paying machine stitchers nearly three times as much as their domestic counterparts, whose pay remained "outrageously low." There would soon be little demand in the industry for women who sewed uppers by hand.

The women workers met and prepared a "high wage list," demanding increased pay for both shop girls and homeworkers. They sought to build an

hand with their own tools, turned the leather into a finished product. Some of the shoemakers were farmers or fishermen who practiced the craft during the slow winter months to augment their regular incomes. Others worked full-time in manufacturing villages, where they labored in corner workrooms inside their homes or in outdoor sheds called ten-footers. But wherever production took place, nearly all male cordwainers relied on wives and daughters to sew or "bind" the upper parts of shoes—a task they performed by hand in their kitchens using a needle and thread.

As the industry expanded in the 1850s, manufacturers found it inefficient to ship materials to homeworkers, who could no longer meet the growing demand. To increase productivity and profits,

Cutting leather for shoes in a Lynn, Massachusetts, factory.

alliance between women factory workers and hand stitchers to create bottlenecks in production.

In subsequent weeks, women conducted their own strike meetings and made their presence felt in the streets. At a March 7, 1860, procession organized in their honor, eight hundred women strikers marched for several hours in falling snow through downtown Lynn, carrying banners that proclaimed their own attachment to the equal rights heritage:

AMERICAN LADIES WILL NOT BE SLAVES: GIVE US A FAIR
COMPENSATION AND WE WILL LABOUR CHEERFULLY

By this time, the great strike attracted national attention. Campaigning for the Republican presidential nomination in New England, Abraham Lincoln declared the walkout a demonstration of the very freedom slavery denied. "I am glad to see that a system of labor prevails in New England under which laborers can strike when they want to, where they are not obliged to labor whether you pay them or not. I like a system which lets a man quit when he wants to, and wish it might prevail everywhere."

Although the men's strike committee actively sought support from women shoeworkers, their proposals did not include any of the demands of either machine stitchers or homeworkers. Afraid that adding the women's grievances to their own would intensify employer resistance, male strike leaders simply ignored the women's demands. Eventually most of the women machine stitchers abandoned the strike, which continued into late March. By this time, the strike was failing and a number of male shoemakers began returning to work. By early April, the employers had won, with only a handful of strikers remaining.

The Civil War required nearly full employment of Massachusetts workers and generated enormous demand for their products—for locomotives from Boston and timepieces from Waltham, boots from Brockton and cotton textiles from New Bedford, woolen goods from Lawrence and leather from Peabody, salted cod from Gloucester and lamp oil from Nantucket, machinery from Hopedale and tools from Athol, wooden ships from Charlestown and rifles from the great Springfield Armory where the "American system" of manufacturing began with the assembly of rifles using interchangeable parts.

By heightening demand for Massachusetts goods, the Civil War accelerated mechanization. For example, from the shoe city of Lynn came this report: "Operatives are pouring in as fast as room can be made for them, buildings for 'shoe factories' are going up in every direction, the hum of machinery is heard on every hand, old things are passing, and all things are becoming new."

The Civil War also elevated the status of working people. The Republican Party of Abraham Lincoln eagerly sought the political support of artisans and mechanics, and many Republican officials in Massachusetts supported demands for the ten-hour and eight-hour day.

During and after the Civil War, new kinds of unity emerged among laboring people in Massachusetts. The war to preserve the Union brought diverse people together in the Grand Army of the Republic. The Irish Ninth Regiment, the Yankee Protestant units, and the black Fifty-fourth all served gallantly in a war that emancipated the slaves and ultimately led to the enfranchisement of black men. The shorter hours movement of the 1860s gained new unity as Irish Catholic workers emerged from their ghettos to lead these struggles and assume prominent leadership roles in trade unions.

For example, Patrick Collins, who came to Boston as a child with parents escaping the "great

"The Shoemakers' Song"

"The Shoemakers' Song" is one of several songs written during the shoemakers' strike. It was written for the strikers by Allen Peabody of Wenham, Massachusetts, and is sung to the tune of "Yankee Doodle."

The Shoemakers' Song

Ye jours and snobs throughout the land,
    'Tis time to be astir;
The Natick boys are all on hand,
    And we must not demur.

    Up and let us have a strike;
    Fair prices we'll demand.
    Firmly let us all unite,
    Unite throughout the land.

This winter past, we've kept alive,
    By toiling late at night.
With no encouragement to thrive—
    Such unpaid toil ain't right.

Starvation looks us in the face,
    We cannot work so low;
Such prices are a sore disgrace;
    Our children ragged go.

Our children must attend the schools,
    And we must pay our bills,
We must have means to buy our tools,
    Gaunt stomachs must be filled.

We must have decent clothes to wear,
    A place to get our rest.
Must not be burdened so with care,
    And must go better dressed.

Are we not men of pluck and nerve?
    Shall we supinely sit,
And starve—another's interest to serve,
    No compensation get?

Shall we run constantly in debt,
    And toil the while like slaves?
Old age may overtake us yet—
    May yet fill pauper's graves.

Shall we saw wood with trembling hands,
    With bowed and aged form?
Beg bread of those whom we've made grand,
    When hoary age comes on?

'Twas union gained the glorious boon,
    Our nation now enjoys;
Then let's awake and soon
    Back up the glorious Natick boys.

Shame on the men, the stupid curs,
    Who might speak if they would,
Who will not join the Union boys,
    But whine, "'Twill do no good."

We are men like other men,
    Must clothe and eat and sleep,
Have dignity and common sense,
    And principles to keep.

The carpenters get up a strike
    The masons do the same,
And we'll take hold with all our might,
    And elevate our name.

'Twas union gained the glorious boon,
    Our nation now enjoys;
Then let's awake and soon
    Back up the glorious Natick boys.

hunger" in Ireland, grew up in Chelsea surrounded by Protestant hostility. Driven from school by anti-Catholic classmates, he became an office boy to a black attorney and schooled himself. Failing to gain apprenticeship as a machinist because of anti-Catholic bias, Collins became an upholsterer, organized a union, and led several strikes during the Civil War. He also served as an organizer for the Irish

Boston Daily Evening Voice

The American Civil War gave birth to the Thirteenth Amendment to the Constitution, which outlawed slavery. With the issuing of the amendment, four million former slaves entered the work force and were greeted with hostility and exploitation at every turn. The organized labor movement in the United States was largely unsympathetic to the plight of these new job seekers. Only one labor newspaper, the *Boston Daily Evening Voice*, advocated the inclusion of former slaves in the labor movement.

The *Voice* was one of at least 130 pro-labor newspapers that sprang into existence during the war. From its beginning in December 1864, it proclaimed that the labor movement must embrace all working people, including women. Furthermore, the *Voice* claimed that if the situation of the American worker improved, then the quality of life for all Americans would improve. The paper also focused, like other labor papers of its time, on issues of education, labor reform, and political action.

In its courageous effort to advocate for the former slaves, the *Voice* appealed to the American workers' sense of reason. The *Voice* echoed a fundamental premise of unionism, stating that only unity without exclusions would result in the fair treatment of all workers. The writers of the *Voice* foresaw that, without organization, former slaves would be given practically nothing for their labor and would be used as strikebreakers. The paper predicted that, eventually, unorganized African American workers would be used to bring down the wages of all working people. The *Voice* rightly claimed that unity alone would prevent such a disaster. The paper urged the labor movement to lead the way in making a reality of America's pledge that all are created equal.

The *Voice* frequently targeted President Andrew Johnson and his policy of not extending citizenship and suffrage to African Americans. The paper argued that former slaves were entitled to political rights. The *Voice* visualized a union of white and African American workers voting together for their rights. Old prejudices and fear of competition from black workers caused unions to look very critically at the position of the *Voice*. Still, the Boston paper refused to alter its position. As a result, the paper lost most of its advertisers and subscribers and ceased publication in October 1867. The labor movement at the time was unable to see the future as clearly as did the *Boston Daily Evening Voice*.

Shaping shoes in a Lynn, Massachusetts, factory.

nationalist movement. After the war, Collins began a political career that would lead from the State House to Boston's City Hall, where he served as the city's second Irish Catholic mayor.

While Irish immigrants such as Collins organized their fellows, Protestant workers began to find new leaders and to broaden their cause. They used the war to extend their political power and to resume the struggle for the shorter working day, a crusade that found a visionary leader in Ira Steward.

Steward served an apprenticeship as a machinist and, while working twelve-hour days, began to agitate for shorter hours. He remained active in the Machinists and Blacksmiths Union and became a full-time agitator for the cause. In 1863, he formed the Boston Eight Hour League. In two years, eight-hour leagues appeared in sixteen other towns and spread to other states. The Charlestown shipyard workers struck to attain the eight-hour day and won the sympathy of President Abraham Lincoln. They elected a ship joiner named Edward H. Rodgers to the legislature in 1864, where he joined a strong group of reformers. The legislature formed Short Time Committees and in 1865 issued a report favoring shorter hours. In the same year, millworkers in Southbridge, Taunton, and New Bedford struck to reduce the working day. And in the elections that

year "eight-hour men" won election to the Lowell and Boston city councils.

To great abolitionists such as Wendell Phillips of Boston, the end of slavery made way for the "next great question for our country—the rights of the laboring class," especially making the eight-hour day a "rule to be observed." In 1867, textile workers in Fall River and New Bedford struck for the ten-hour day. But the promising eight-hour movement faced frustration when the legislature refused to enact statewide legislation. It would take many more decades of struggle and much more effective organization to make the eight-hour day a reality.

As a result of the Civil War, free labor triumphed over slave labor. But the meaning of freedom remained unclear to men, women, and children who still toiled for ten and twelve hours daily in the Commonwealth's workplaces. George McNeill, a co-founder of the Boston Eight Hour League, argued that employers set the terms of labor contracts and decided what constituted a "fair day's work" and a "fair day's pay." To McNeill and other pioneers of the Massachusetts labor movement, such a dictatorial system had no place in a republic founded on principles of democracy and equal rights, principles for which more than half a million died on Civil War battlefields.

PART III

THE CALL FOR SOLIDARITY, 1866-1901

THE CIVIL WAR CREATED NEW OPPORTUNI-ties for Massachusetts workers. But to take advantage of these changes, workers would need new and different organizations. After the war, workers expressed a desire to organize across various dividing lines at both the national and the local level. The National Labor Union, formed in 1864, issued a new call for solidarity among working people, and in early conventions NLU leader William Sylvis made stirring appeals for the equal rights of women and blacks.

The first signs of the new labor movement in Massachusetts appeared in Fall River, where women weavers and male spinners organized powerful associations. Later, beginning in the shoe towns and spreading across the Commonwealth and the nation, the Knights and the Daughters of St. Crispin were formed as new and powerful unions.

The collapse of these new organizations during the long depression of the 1870s only heightened workers' desire for a stronger labor movement. Across the country workers' uprisings were taking place—uprisings increasingly met with violence and repression. In the Pennsylvania coalfields, for example, the Irish Molly Maguires who tried to organize were framed by company guards and hanged. In the bloody railroad strike of 1877, militia fired on workers and their supporters, causing nearly one hundred deaths in a number of local conflicts. As workers struck to defend their wages and their

rights, social elites, reacting hysterically, warned of revolution.

In Fall River, an uprising of the city's weavers and spinners ended in 1875, after months of struggle, when the governor ordered the militia to enter the city and allowed employers to fire union workers and reopen the mills on their own terms. In order to regain their jobs, the city's proud British workers were forced to sign "yellow dog contracts" pledging to quit their unions. But they did not consider these contracts binding "as it was their starving children that compelled them to sign . . . against their wills." "An empty stomach can make no contracts," George McNeill wrote.

Even after the depression ended, workers worried gravely about their working conditions. Mechanization continued to displace skilled workers and drove the remainder beyond human limits. More and more women and children were forced into factories and sweatshops. Carroll Wright, the commissioner of the state's Bureau of Labor Statistics, in 1873 wrote that at least twenty-five thousand children were "growing up without any, or but the slightest knowledge of the rudiments of education."

There have been times in American labor history when workers, long deprived of dignity and justice, confronted employers in open conflict. Known as the Great Upheaval, the mid-1880s witnessed an extraordinary outpouring of worker militancy. Four hundred forty-three work stoppages were recorded in 1884, but 1,432 erupted in 1886, when more than four hundred thousand American workers surged into the streets.

The Noble Order of the Knights of Labor played a central role in this uprising. Founded in 1869 by Philadelphia garment cutters, the Order was for many years a secret society. By 1882, the Knights abandoned secrecy and began operating in the open, yet they had only forty thousand members. But all this changed during the Great Upheaval. Between July 1, 1885, and June 30, 1886, membership increased sevenfold, climbing to nearly 750,000.

The Knights of Labor arose from the agony of the 1870s holding up a vision of a Cooperative Commonwealth—a vision of a society based on democracy and cooperation. Abhorring conflict and violence, leaders such as the Grand Master Workman Terence Powderly advocated for arbitration over strikes, cooperation between labor and owners, and the creation of workers' cooperatives to produce goods.

Almost paralyzed by their lofty goals, the Knights watched their membership grow restless and impatient and ultimately leave in favor of rival organizations. In Massachusetts, many would leave to join the American Federation of Labor (AFL), as did former Knights of Labor leader Frank Foster. AFL craft unionism in some respects marked the return

for many Massachusetts workers to earlier experiments with trade unionism. The AFL embraced a "pure and simple unionism" as Samuel Gompers would call it, or what others would call "bread and butter unionism." Yet in Massachusetts, the AFL also retained parts of the vision advanced by the Knights and Crispins. The federation would change many times before it merged with the Congress of Industrial Organizations (CIO) in 1955, but Massachusetts workers enjoyed, for the first time, a permanent organization to represent their interests.

At the same time, building trades across the Commonwealth were organizing. Given the seasonal and often temporary nature of employment, building trades workers faced very different conditions than their sisters in the textile mills or their brothers in the crafts. In cities such as Boston and Holyoke, the building trades sprouted from ethnic communities. Building trades unions themselves were often direct outgrowths of ethnic associations. Still, they often found themselves in conflict with the leaders of their own communities, who owned and controlled contracting. And while it would be another generation before many of the trades would become fully organized, the tradesmen's pride in their work and their tenacity of spirit became another force for the workers' movement in the Commonwealth and the nation.

CHAPTER 6

The Crispins and the Knights of Labor

URING AND AFTER THE CIVIL WAR, MASSACHU-setts labor reformers gained political experience while factory workers learned from their organizational failures before the war. By the late 1860s, reform leaders had pushed the labor question to the center of public debate and workers formed powerful new union organizations.

The most influential of these new movements was the Knights of St. Crispin, conceived in 1864 by Newell Daniels, a shoe worker from Milford, Massachusetts. The Crispins grew to seventy thousand members by 1870, when they spread beyond the Commonwealth to other New England states. Their base broadened in 1869 as women stitchers formed the Daughters of St. Crispin. At the Daughters' first convention in Lynn, the leaders of the Knights pledged the votes of thirty thousand Crispin men in favor of women's suffrage.

When their lodges met to celebrate in 1869, work halted in shoe towns across the state and there were picnics, parades, and speeches by local officials. A report from Abington commented that, along with Crispin banners showing a muscular arm holding a shoemaker's hammer, "flew American and Irish flags, typical of the unity of race and feeling on the occasion." These celebrations, writes historian David Montgomery, "made it unmistakably clear that the labor reform movement had established itself by the end of the Civil War decade as a force to be reckoned with in American political and economic life."

The Crispins became powerful enough in Massa-chusetts to strike successfully for higher wages for all levels of workers in the shoe industry. In shoe towns such as Lynn, the call for solidarity had been answered and unity produced a better life for working people. In Marlborough, an influential citizen told the Bureau of Labor Statistics: "There are those who think the organization of the Knights of St. Crispins works to the injury of our town. I think otherwise." Belonging to the union allowed shoe workers to stay in town, to shop there, and to buy homes rather than be transient. He continued, "The interest of the working people in town is increased. . . . and Marlborough is in every way more prosperous than it would have been but for the labor movement."

At the state level, the Crispins lobbied the legislators to create a Bureau of Labor Statistics in 1869. The Bureau, the first in the nation, was headed by Boston labor reformer George McNeill. It produced many valuable studies of the status of working people in the Commonwealth, research that helped advance the 1874 law limiting to ten hours the workday of women and children in manufacturing.

The Crispins helped found a Labor Reform Party in 1870, headed by gubernatorial candidate Wendell Phillips, the state's most important reformer. The labor movement aimed to do much more than improve wages and hours in the trades. It sought to reform the Commonwealth and save it from being captured by "Class-Wealth."

The Crispins became so effective that employers

Members of the Knights of Labor, displaying their tools.

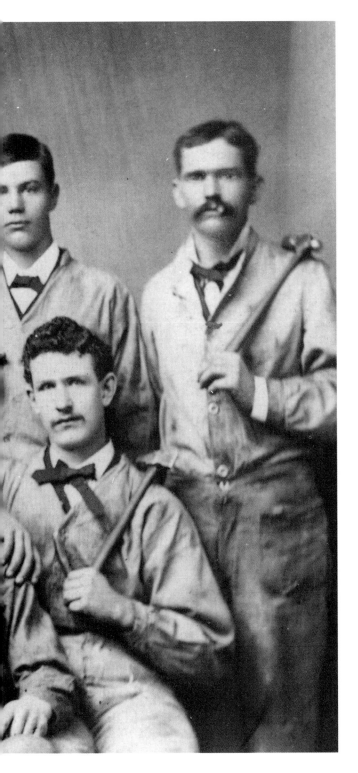

counterattacked. In 1872 they cut wages and launched a frontal assault on the Crispins, locking them out of the shoe shops. They then refused to hire any union members in their factories, effectively blacklisting them. Already weakened by this attack, the Crispins did not survive the terrible depression that hit in 1873.

But even before these hard times, disunity appeared. The Crispins espoused the notion of equal rights of workers, yet they extended the logic of solidarity only so far—often excluding women and people of color. For example, when shoe bosses brought Chinese immigrants to break a strike in North Adams, the union asserted that the strike-breakers had no rights. "The Crispins failed . . . because, while seeking justice for their own members, they failed to be just to the workers outside their fold," labor leader Frank Foster concluded in 1887.

When the cruel depression relented in the late 1870s, a new national organization, the Noble and Holy Order of the Knights of Labor, rose to renew the call for solidarity and to develop new methods for assuring unity. The Knights' motto, "An Injury to One Is the Concern of All," signaled their inclusiveness. In addition to welcoming laborers and unskilled mill workers, the Order sought to overcome longstanding barriers of race and gender as well. As veterans of the antislavery movement, prominent Knights such as Bay State reformer George McNeill deplored working-class racism and remained staunch advocates of racial equality. Nationally, 166 local assemblies were established by African Americans. Although a Marblehead boot and shoe cutters' lodge was the only completely black Massachusetts local, individual black workers belonged to other assemblies.

The Knights' national leaders were equally strong proponents of women's equality. "The rights of the sexes are co-equal," Grand Master Workman Terence Powderly stated, and male workers should give women their cooperation "as a right to which they are entitled by reason of the nobility of toil no matter by whom performed." Even more noteworthy was the Knights' broad definition of women's work. When Powderly spoke of the "nobility of toil," he drew no distinction between household and wage labor. He believed that all forms of work demanded the same respect. The Order not only supported

Women delegates to the General Assembly of the Knights of Labor in Richmond, Virginia, in October 1886.

The letterhead of the Knights of Labor.

women's demands for equal pay but opened its doors to the homebound wives and daughters of workingmen.

The Knights' message was heartily welcomed by Bay State women. North Adams weavers, Beverly buttonholers, and Taunton and Fall River textile workers all formed women's lodges. In Danville, women in the Knights established a cooperative underwear factory. As with male workers, support was especially strong in shoe towns, where women stitchers had a long history of collective action and needed little prompting to form their own organizations. The list of local assemblies included lodges in Beverly, Haverhill, Lynn, Marblehead, Marlborough, Natick, North Adams, Salem, and Stoneham. Many of these women embraced the Order's aims with the same unflinching dedication that stitchers had earlier exhibited as members of the Daughters of St. Crispin. "Sisters," a Lynn "union girl" declared, "we undertook a life work when we enrolled our names on the 'Knights of Labor' records; then let us stand firm and unwavering while we know our cause is just."

The Knights espoused cooperation with employers, favored arbitration over strikes, and pledged to use the democratic process to achieve their ends. Unwilling to accept the wage system, they imagined a cooperative commonwealth in which economic life, like political life, would be organized democratically. Indeed, the Knights even denied the employer-employee dichotomy. Like earlier artisans in Massachusetts, they believed that all workers were producers and were therefore entitled to equal rights. The Knights respected private property but hated those who monopolized land and wealth. They wanted an economy organized upon principles affirming that all citizens enjoyed an equal right to independence and a decent livelihood.

As an alternative to competitive capitalism and the wage system, the Knights boldly set out a vision for a cooperative commonwealth in which workers could produce goods in their own shops and sell them directly to the public. Leaders such as Terence Powderly abhorred class conflict and the class politics preached by socialists. The Knights intended to use the institutions of government against employers who refused to treat workers fairly.

By 1885 the Order had mobilized workers to demand reform from the legislature. That year the leader of the statewide Knights of Labor District 30,

Robert Howard, won the first of eight terms in the state senate from Fall River. Soon labor reforms emerged from legislative committees and many of them became law as the Democratic Party adopted a pro-worker agenda and acted for a while as a kind of labor party.

The eight-hour day remained the Knights' central demand. In early 1886 this crusade helped attract thousands of new members into District 30, which became the largest state organization in the nation. Many officials viewed the Order's expansion as a mixed blessing and were concerned about the new members. Some were particularly alarmed by the rash of work stoppages that had fueled extraordinary growth. "Judging from some of the reports in the *Journal* [*of United Labor*]," Albert A. Carlton, head of Massachusetts District Assembly 30, remarked, "many Districts as well as locals imagine that to strike is our highest aim and that to win a strike the greatest victory that could be achieved. Instruction seems to be badly needed."

The militancy of the Great Upheaval culminated on May 1, 1886, when thousands of union workers and others struck for the eight-hour day. The great strike had been proposed by Frank Foster, a printer from Haverhill, Massachusetts, who had been an important leader of the Knights. Foster had joined other craft unionists in founding a new federation of trade unions in 1881 and then later calling for a general strike to win the eight-hour day. These trade unionists maintained membership in the Knights but objected to the non-confrontational stance of its leaders. On May 1, the Boston building trades led the dramatic strike for the eight-hour day after declaring: "This is the workingman's hour and affrighted capital begins to understand that labor has rights it is bound to respect."

The Knights opposed the walkout but many of

Massachusetts Knights of Labor leader Henry Charles Litchman.

their members struck anyway, denouncing their timid leaders. Many left the Order, discouraged by the Knights' inability to confront anti-union employers and expressing doubt about the grand reform vision of creating a cooperative alternative to the capitalist wage system. The craftsmen who had been loyal to the Knights when they seemed invincible now turned to the independent trade assemblies affiliated with the new American Federation of Labor. Its leaders offered a militant but pragmatic strategy for building permanent unions based on occupational solidarity. But the Knights did not disappear immediately, nor did their dream of what George McNeill called "one great solidarity."

How Massachusetts Workers Lived

In 1874, officials of the Massachusetts Bureau of Statistics of Labor (MBSL) conducted a major survey of nearly 400 worker households. Their findings, published in the bureau's 1875 report, revealed the differing fortunes of Bay State working people as revealed in their annual incomes.

No. 10   CARPENTER

EARNINGS of father,	$716
son, aged 15,	300
	$1,016

CONDITION.—Family numbers six, parents and four children from four to sixteen years of age; two go to school, including the eldest girl, who also helps the mother at home. Occupy a tenement of six rooms pleasantly situated, with agreeable surroundings and a small flower-garden attached. The house is well furnished and parlor carpeted. Own a piano and sewing-machine. Family dresses well and attends church.

FOOD.—*Breakfast.* Bread and butter, meat or fish, cake, tea.
Dinner. Bread and butter, meat, potatoes, vegetables, pickles, pie or pudding.
Supper. Bread, butter, cold corned meat, doughnuts, or gingerbread, cheese and tea. Baked beans Sunday morning.

COST OF LIVING			$981
Rent	$200.00	Fish	$12.00
Dry goods	30.50	Fuel	50.75
Milk	33.26	Papers	8.00
Groceries	356.00	Shoes	27.80
Religion	12.00	Meat	114.64
Clothing	107.00	Sundries	29.05

No. 219   LABORER, IN MILL

EARNINGS of father,	$382
son, aged 10,	190
	$572

CONDITION.—Family numbers six, parents and four children from nine months to ten years of age; one goes to school. Have a tenement of four rooms in an eight-tenement block, with one door on the front and none on the back; the locality and surroundings unclean and disagreeable. The privy is within six feet of the building. The inside of the house is as dirty as the surroundings, and very poorly furnished. Family is poor.

FOOD.—*Breakfast.* Pork or salt fish, potatoes, bread and coffee.
Dinner. Meat, potatoes, sometimes vegetables, and bread.
Supper. Bread, butter, sometimes gingerbread, and tea. Fish for dinner, instead of meat, two days in the week.

COST OF LIVING			$572
Rent	$84.00	Fish	$18.60
Fuel	29.50	Milk	12.00
Groceries	273.25	Shoes	14.80
Meat	47.92	Clothing	27.00
Dry goods	11.50	Sundries	53.43

CHAPTER 7

The American Federation of Labor

WE CAN FOLLOW THE BIRTH OF THE AMERican Federation of Labor in Massachusetts through the pages of Frank Foster's *Labor Leader*, which began publication in 1887. A printer by trade, the Thorndike, Massachusetts–born Foster went east to Boston during the early 1880s. Elected president of the Boston Typographical Union in 1882, he figured prominently in both the craft-dominated Boston Central Labor Union (CLU) and the Knights of Labor. From 1883 to 1886, he edited the Order's *Haverhill Laborer*, and attained executive rank in District Assembly 30. By the following year, though, Foster's commitment to the Knights was clearly on the wane and his editorials in the *Labor Leader* strongly suggested that the Order had outlived its usefulness.

The main problem, as he saw it, was the Knights' policy of "forming bodies of no distinctive trade character, where the principle of self-interest was assumed to be so far subordinated that men of different callings would legislate wisely and impartially for one another." According to Foster, "men occupied at the same calling have more interests in common than men in diverse trades." That being the case, he proposed that the Knights be restructured along craft lines, focusing on concrete workplace issues. After all, he observed, "Business is business, [and] our business in a labor society is higher wages, shorter hours, and greater liberties for the wage workers." Dismissing the Knights' broader reform agenda, Foster declared that workers were "tiring of moonbeam soup" and what they wanted was "bigger slices of bread and butter and more beefsteak." If the Order could not move beyond what he called the "hurrah period of the American labor movement," then it would be left behind.

The masthead of the *Labor Leader*, the official publication of the Massachusetts AFL, edited by Frank Foster.

Foster's remarks constitute a clear statement of the model of pure and simple unionism posited by Samuel Gompers and the AFL. It was no surprise that, during the summer of 1887, Foster played a leading role in the formation of the Massachusetts chapter of the AFL, the labor organization that fully embodied these principles. Foster had mixed feelings about the Knights' policy of inclusiveness. On one hand, he believed it hampered the development of craft unionism. Yet, on the other, he realized that it was an expression of lofty ideals that no union of workers should ever completely abandon. And with the new direction the AFL signaled, he worried that labor's "general unity of purpose is apt to be forgotten."

The practical tactics of the trade unions created durable organizations that, for the first time in labor history, survived a major depression. By 1895, the AFL grew rapidly as craft unions, led by the building trades, extended to cities and towns all over the Commonwealth. Beyond the earliest building-trades unions—the carpenters, bricklayers, painters, and plasterers—new construction unions formed in the 1890s, including the electricians, sheet metal workers, iron workers, and hod carriers, to name a few. Together with the craft unions in the construction trades, skilled workers reorganized powerful trade unions in the railroad, printing, metalworking, iron-molding, shoe, textile, and cigar-making industries. Craft unions also formed among bartenders and waiters, musicians, bakers, and other tradesmen.

Craftsmen usually expressed their pride and self-worth by asserting their "manhood" against bosses who would belittle them. Their unions were "brotherhoods" with rules and rituals that bonded workingmen together. But these union halls and lodges, like the workingmen's saloons, excluded women, who were supposed to stay home.

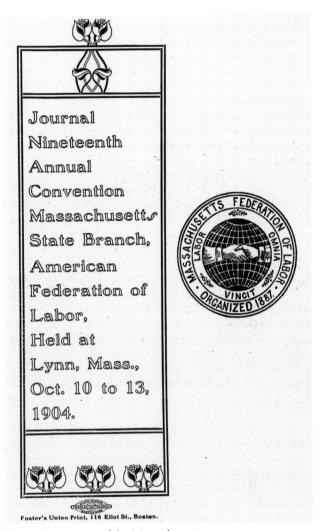

From the program of the Massachusetts AFL convention in 1904.

Compared with the position adopted by the Knights, AFL policy on organizing African Americans, women, and unskilled workers was considerably less inclusive. The Federation endorsed the widely held view that only men should be breadwinners—the sole supporters of their families—and thus they discouraged females from entering their trades or joining their unions. AFL affiliates also supported immigration restriction and set up barriers to membership for foreign-born workers. Many

HOME OF THE SCAB WORKMAN

THE HOME OF THE UNION WORKMAN.

This illustration of the benefits of belonging to a union appeared
in the October 6, 1894, edition of the *Labor Leader*.

blatantly excluded blacks through "white only" membership clauses. Moreover, craft unionists often adopted the widespread and vicious stereotypes of African Americans and Asians and of immigrants from southern and eastern Europe.

But not all AFL unions excluded unskilled workers or ethnic minorities. The hod carriers organized a powerful trade union, first among Irish immigrants and then among Italian laborers. Immigrants from Italy who found themselves in bondage to labor bosses rallied around a union formed by Domenic D'Alessandro of Boston's North End. The Brewery Workers Union, led by German socialists, insisted on organizing all workers in the industry, including beer-wagon drivers, even though it brought them into conflict with the Teamsters union.

Other craft unions also amalgamated and opened their membership to less-skilled workers. For example, the International Ladies' Garment Workers' Union formed as the skilled male cutters amalgamated with female locals of sewers and pressers. A new union, the Boot and Shoe Workers, formed in shoe manufacturing towns in 1895, incorporating male locals of lasters and cutters with female locals of stitchers.

While significantly less inclusive than the Knights, the Federation nevertheless mounted ambitious programs to reach out to all workers in Massachusetts. A good example is the federation's union label program. AFL leaders reasoned that if working people could be persuaded to buy only union-made goods, their purchasing power would add substantially to the bargaining strength of organized workers. The Massachusetts campaign began in 1890 at a meeting of the Joint Label Conference of New England. Afterward, cigar makers regularly checked saloon shelves for union-made cigars; United Garment Workers members inspected the

apparel in clothing stores for the union label; and Central Labor Unions enforced national boycotts of various goods produced by "unfair" manufacturers.

Unorganized wage earners benefited as well. Informed of the abysmal working conditions of women clerks in Boston stores, the *Labor Leader*'s editor suggested that this was "one of the cases where the efficacy of a public boycott ought to be tried in bringing the wealthy proprietors to a sense of their duty toward their employees."

Even though the AFL undertook limited organizational efforts outside its base of skilled male workers, a growing number of less-skilled workers created unions of their own. As the economy revived after the terrible depression of the 1890s, working people from all segments of the labor force banded together to demand restoration of wages that had been cut and other concessions made during hard times. The ensuing organizational boom extended well beyond the ranks of AFL craftsmen.

In Boston the legislature bowed to the labor movement, making Labor Day an official state holiday. On September 5, 1887, more than twenty thousand workers marched through the streets of the capital in a well-ordered procession celebrating their freedom day. "It was a grand pageant," wrote the *Boston Globe*, "a veritable festival of joy . . . recognized by the people of Boston and vicinity." Later, in Holyoke in 1901, twenty-five thousand people lined local thoroughfares to watch six thousand workers, ranging from "the humble bootblack to the skilled laborer," parade through the streets of the Paper City. Similar scenes occurred in cities and towns throughout the Commonwealth.

In the state's largest city, trade unionism flourished in the late 1890s when the Boston Central Labor Union became a powerful force representing nearly all of organized labor. It adjudicated disputes,

This advertisement from November 25, 1893, was one
of many that appeared in the pages of the *Labor Leader*
encouraging its readers to buy union products.

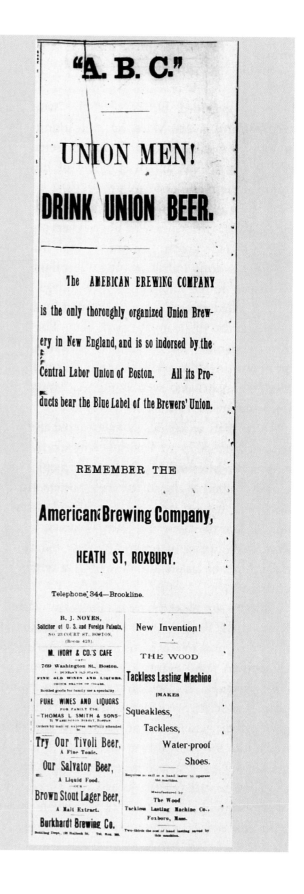

called for consumer boycotts, and secured government action on behalf of all workers. Moreover,
organized labor won public support not only from
social reformers and clergy but from merchants and
professionals. As settlement house pioneer Robert
Woods wrote in 1898, "Each year marks the growth
of trade-union sympathy among the people."

This sympathy aroused support from Democratic
politicians including state legislator John "Honey
Fitz" Fitzgerald of the North End and young James
Michael Curley in Roxbury, who eagerly sought the
labor vote and supported the labor reforms champi-
oned by Mayor Josiah Quincy in 1897. Attempting
to restore trade unions' faith in his party, which had
been badly shaken by the Democrats' failure to help
the unemployed, Quincy made sure city contracts
went to union workers. Indeed, he opened a city
printing plant staffed by union members, and in
1899 the city enacted an eight-hour day for its
employees, a goal unions had struggled to achieve
since before the Civil War. The "great improvement
in all the conditions of labor," Robert Woods
concluded, was entirely "the result of working-class
organization."

At a national level, AFL membership stood at
265,000 in 1897, but by 1904 total union membership exceeded 2 million. Dramatic union gains also
took place in the Commonwealth. The Massachusetts State Federation of Labor, formed in 1887, grew
from a body representing 42 local unions and city-
based labor councils in 1897 to representation of 115
affiliates in 1907.

The Federation, led by Frank Foster on Beacon
Hill, acted on an ambitious legislative agenda that

Frank K. Foster: Labor's Intellectual and Reformer

Frank Foster, leader of the Knights of Labor and the AFL in Massachusetts.

A printer by trade and a member of Boston's Typographical Union 13, Frank K. Foster became one of labor's voices for social reform toward the end of the nineteenth century. In the 1880s, he held important posts in the Knights of Labor. Following that organization's decline, he went on to serve as the secretary of the AFL with Samuel Gompers, P. J. McGuire, and Adolphe Strasser. Foster was also a founder of the Bay State's Federa-tion of Labor, holding office as secretary and later as chair of the legislative committee.

The printer became known for his unique philosophy of social reform when, in 1887, he became editor of the *Labor Leader*, the official paper for trade unions in the Bay State and Boston. In the editorials and news stories he penned, as well as in his poetry and short stories, his identity as an artisan in a craft union signifi-cantly shaped his outlook. His "collective indi-vidualism" was a means by which individual workers emancipated themselves by improving their social and cultural standing. Working-class liberal artisans such as Foster valued this kind of self-reliance, yet industrial production and the unfair advantages enjoyed by the rich had eroded their social standing as independent craftsmen. For Foster, trade unionism meant achieving for workers the rights and privileges formerly monopolized by the few. To realize these goals, though, political activity was required.

As head of the legislative committee of the Massachusetts State Federation of Labor, he demanded that the legislature ban such abuses as yellow-dog contracts, Pinkertonism, sweatshops, and the exploitation of the labor of women and children. He also called for municipal owner-ship of the railroads and telegraphs because as monopolies they impeded individual action. Due to his conviction that trade unions should main-tain their independence from political parties, even those specifically oriented toward the work-ing class, his legislative program was promoted by supporting candidates from both of the major parties or even third-party candidates who supported his program for reform.

kept Massachusetts in the forefront in developing progressive labor laws. The AFL continued to demand a humane working day. In 1890, the legislature passed a nine-hour law for state employees, and in 1906 it enacted an eight-hour law for state mechanics and laborers. In 1911, legislators reduced the work week of textile workers to fifty-four hours. Two years later Massachusetts adopted the Uniform Child Labor Law which excluded minors from many dangerous jobs and reduced the work day to eight hours for children between fourteen and sixteen years of age.

Many of the pioneering health and safety laws in Massachusetts were strengthened during this period, and in 1904 the State Board of Health was required to inspect workplaces. In 1911, the Federation successfully modified the original Workmen's Compensation Act, and in 1913 it helped create a new Board of Labor and Industries and an Industrial Accident Board to institutionalize state regulation of workplace health and safety. A year later, the AFL celebrated the passage of a law requiring the Board of Labor to make sure government contractors paid wages at a scale "not less than the customary and prevailing rate of wages for a day's work at the same trade or occupation."

This kind of political influence was a direct outgrowth of union strength and solidarity in cities such as Brockton, where by 1910 an amazing 59.7 percent of the work force belonged to the Boot and Shoe Workers and other AFL unions. Other strong union cities included Lynn (25.5 percent), Quincy (22.8 percent), Boston (21.1 percent), and Springfield (17.8 percent). However, the level of unionization across the state stood at a modest 11 percent, about the national average. Major industrial cities such as

Taunton, Pittsfield, and Worcester averaged only 10 percent. "Through the system of spying and black listing in vogue . . ." wrote the *Worcester Labor News* in 1915, "even the thought of belonging to a union made a man in danger of losing his job."

Despite public sympathy and political influence, organized labor in Boston faced tough opposition from hard-nosed employers. The city's revived labor movement faced a crisis in 1912 when the workers on the Boston Elevated engaged in a critical strike. The Elevated's owners discharged the leaders and provoked a strike of 3,800 operators that spread to Cambridge, Somerville, and other towns. The company hired two thousand strikebreakers and violent clashes erupted on many lines. The police mercilessly beat strikers, but failed to discourage them. Public support grew as thousands walked to and from work instead of riding "scab cars."

The city council, spurred by trade union member James Moriarity, condemned the company and called upon Mayor John Fitzgerald to take action. "Honey Fitz" helped to secure a settlement as did Democratic Governor Eugene Foss, who with labor's support had defeated the anti-union Republican incumbent in 1910. As a result, Local 589 of the Amalgamated Transit Union established itself as an influential force in the Boston labor movement.

By the turn of the century the AFL had become an important power in the Commonwealth's economic and political life. Indeed, its affiliates had endured the terrible depression of the 1890s to become important, active organizations. They kept the "labor question" on the public agenda and scored important achievements for working people through direct action and through the use of local and state government.

CHAPTER 8

Irish Immigrants Build Holyoke

In the Connecticut River valley, in the western part of the state, Holyoke grew dramatically in the middle of the nineteenth century. Before the 1840s, it had been a tiny village called Ireland Parish. Most of its inhabitants were farmers who grew hay, corn, rye, potatoes, and oats on its fertile bottomlands. Its major enterprise was a small cotton mill that employed fewer than seventy workers. This began to change in 1846 when the state's expanding railroad network finally reached the area. Holyoke then attracted a group of eastern capitalists, the same Boston Associates who built the Lowell mills.

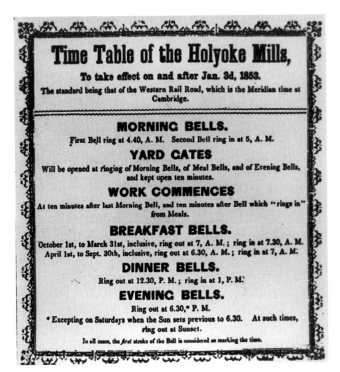

This schedule gives an idea of the hours that were worked in the 1850s.

What made the area so appealing was the industrial potential of Hadley Falls, where the swiftly moving waters of the Connecticut dropped nearly sixty feet. A dam was planned for the site, and a series of canals were envisioned that could supply water power to a number of new mills.

Upon the dam's completion in November 1848, crowds of interested onlookers lined the Connecticut to witness the grand opening. If they were seeking a spectacle, the ensuing events provided enough excitement for everybody. Shortly after the last gates on the newly erected structure were closed, problems developed. At noon, company officials telegraphed Boston that "the dam is leaking badly." A further message an hour later evinced mounting panic: "We cannot stop the leaking." Things only got worse. The final telegram Boston investors received that afternoon simply read: "Dam gone to hell by way of Willimansett."

Although a second dam proved successful, industrial development proceeded slowly. Only a handful of mills went up before 1857, and with that year's economic panic construction ceased altogether. Not until the Civil War years did Holyoke show signs of becoming a major manufacturing center, thanks to government contracts, high tariffs, and soaring prices. These factors provided a solid foundation for the growth of several newly constructed textile mills, but the war boom also spurred expansion of the city's fledgling paper industry. By 1870, Holyoke was no longer the rural backwater it had been at midcentury. Its population had tripled to 10,733, and the town's eleven paper mills employed more than a

Construction of Parson's Paper Mill No. 2 in the Churchill Section of Holyoke on the second level canal. The mill is still in operation.

thousand workers who produced tissue paper, book-quality paper, and the fine white writing paper that would make Holyoke famous. A decade later the population had again doubled, and, with increasing industrial activity, the city would continue to grow for another forty years.

These developments meant work and opportunity for a broad range of local residents. Nowhere was this more important than in the city's Irish community. Arriving shortly before midcentury, Holyoke's earliest Irish settlers came from the famine-ravaged southwestern counties of their suffering homeland. Forced to live in crowded and unsanitary work camps, they found employment as laborers on the dam, dug canals that ran through Holyoke, and helped construct the first mills. Despite miserable conditions, many persisted. As early as 1855, the Irish made up more than one-third of Holyoke's population. They would remain the city's dominant ethnic group for decades to come.

Although many Irish immigrants subsequently worked in local factories, a substantial number continued to find employment in construction. Where in 1860 three of every four skilled construction workers were Yankees, they held fewer than 20 percent of these positions two decades later. And as they moved out, the Irish moved in. They also moved up. Employment as a carpenter, bricklayer, or stonemason represented real mobility for someone who might otherwise have been digging ditches or carrying hods. In some instances, individuals achieved prominence as contractors. Such was the case of Maurice Lynch, who was born in County Kerry in 1837 and came to the United States a decade later when the potato rot devastated his homeland. As a boy, he apprenticed as a brickmaker and later formed a successful contracting business with his brothers.

But the life of a building tradesman was far from easy. In addition to the physical hardships and injuries that went with the job, construction workers faced constant economic insecurity. Where some jobs took years to complete, others ended in a few weeks, and building tradesmen often worried about when the next layoff was coming and how long it would last. "There is no such thing as steady employment in the building trades," one observer remarked. "There never was and never will be until the skies stop leading snow and rain."

For all this, most building tradesmen loved what they did. Not only were they among the highest paid wage earners during this time, their strong sense of craft pride helped them deal with the irregular employment cycles and other adverse features of construction work. The results of their labor were there for everyone to view, and all of them at one time or another shared the feelings of Walter Stevenson, a twentieth-century union carpenter: "As I pass up and down [my city's] streets I see in many places the work my own hands have wrought on her buildings and I feel that in a sense I am a part of our city. My strength and whatever skill I possess are woven into her material fabric that will remain when I am gone, for Labor is Life taking a permanent form."

Although this sense of achievement provided some compensation for daily hardships on the job, building tradesmen knew that craft pride would not improve working conditions. At various times throughout the century, they had formed organizations to combat contractor injustices and regulate employment practices. But until the 1880s, none of these organizations lasted. This time it was different.

A number of the construction unions created during that decade would take their place among the most powerful and enduring organizations in the American labor movement. Within Massachusetts, Holyoke building tradesmen were in the front ranks of these campaigns. Local bricklayers led the way, followed shortly afterward by the carpenters, who in 1881 received the first charter issued to Bay State workers by the recently formed Brotherhood of Carpenters and Joiners. Not far behind were the painters and other crafts.

A major objective of these organizations was to control the labor market in their respective trades. But as long as employers could draw on sizable pools of nonunion workers for construction projects, building craftsmen would never attain the economic security they so desperately sought. Nonunion workers also undermined any leverage the organized workers might have in work stoppages or strikes. These concerns, as well as a determination to maintain the work standards that were the basis of craft pride, made apprenticeship a matter of vital importance to construction unionists. Although relatively few workers participated in formal training programs, those wishing to get union cards did have to demonstrate proficiency in their craft. And by limiting the number of cards issued, unionists hoped to regulate the supply of journeymen in a given labor market.

A key figure in these early organizations, particularly in the carpenters' locals, was the "walking delegate." As chief disciplinarian, he brought charges against members who violated union rules and regulations. As business manager, he kept the books and collected dues. As head negotiator, he represented members at bargaining sessions with contractors. When he was not performing these duties, he could most often be found at local building sites, where he listened to worker grievances and insured that employers were not using nonunion labor. He was not another boss but their delegate, and they counted on him to help keep employers in line. Their sentiments were perhaps best expressed by the Holyoke carpenter who, during an 1892 labor dispute, declared: "We should also like to know by what particular right or privilege the contractor presumes to buy lumber that is not chopped by union choppers, drawn by union teamsters, sawed by union sawyers, planed by union planers, and approved by our walking delegate whom we pay to do nothing but go around and find out what they can about the contractor's business and report to us so we can regulate the things."

As the new organizations took shape, they created their own culture. Particular emphasis was placed on the importance of cooperation and solidarity. Such values were hardly new to Irish workers, who had grown up in tightly knit ethnic communities where neighbors routinely did what they could to assist each other. It was nevertheless vital for members to develop new loyalties and begin to think of themselves as trade unionists as well as Irishmen. To speed the process, unions sponsored public meetings at which speakers provided instruction in trade union

Brick workers building a kiln for firing bricks at the Lynch Brothers' brickyards. They supplied most of the brick for local mills and apartments.

A trench is being cut in the bedrock with steam drills. This allowed the base of the Holyoke dam to be set into the bedrock and firmly anchored to the riverbed.

principles. Unions also took over a number of the functions traditionally performed by ethnic organizations. These included payment for funerals and maintenance of sick-benefit funds, as well as the organization of entertainment committees that sponsored dances and other social events. Construction unionists further practiced solidarity by providing financial assistance to striking workers in other locals.

Between 1880 and 1905, building trades unions participated in almost three times as many strikes as workers in any other industry. The trades in Holyoke were no exception. As the ground softened each spring and construction began, employers and unionists squared off against each other in what by the late 1880s had become an annual ritual. Workers initiated the confrontation by issuing their demands and requiring a response by May 1, a carefully chosen date that gave workers time to replenish savings accounts with the new construction season. For the next month, typically, little happened. Then, in late April, both sides announced their readiness to do battle, and newspapers published the gloomy predictions of local realtors who invariably foresaw a dismal building season if unionists did not accept the contractors' terms.

The mounting tensions of these final days sometimes exposed divisions within Holyoke's previously united Irish community. In April 1888, for example, when union bricklayers declared that they would strike if they were not given a wage increase, management chose Maurice Lynch as their main spokesman. Lynch knew many of the bricklayers well. Besides attending the same church they did, he was

A dangerous job

Submarine divers on the Holyoke Dam pose for this photo taken in 1885, the same year The Holyoke Daily Transcript reported two divers killed, one on June 8 and another on July 17. The photo was taken and published by W.P. Warner of Holyoke

Oracle

Life wasn't easy for divers on the Holyoke Dam, despite the relative tranquility depicted in the photograph above.

Through research done by Holyoke Water Power Co., we learned that this crew was hired by the utility in the spring and summer of 1885 to investigate the condition of the wooden dam as part of a repair project.

The accompanying two news reports from the then Holyoke Daily Transcript (predecessor of the Transcript-Telegram) show that work was dangerous and sometimes fatal.

Holyoke Daily Transcript
June 8, 1885

The Diver's Death
He Goes Over the Dam

George Constine of East Boston, the professional diver who has been employed at the dam and whose operations were recently described in the Transcript, was killed this morning at 9 o'clock. In his air-tight, brass armour, loaded with his heavy brass shoes and leaden belt, he had dived to the bottom of the river above the dam and crawled up on the inside slope to the crest. The water stood three feet deep at that point, the flash boards having been removed, and the current was very strong. He was washed over the dam, and the tender allowed the rope he was holding, and which was attached to diver's waist, to pay entirely out. In his other hand the tender held the air hose through which the diver received his supply of air. As the rope ran out a strain came on the air-hose, and it snapped in two. The diver went down the apron. The body was recovered in five minutes but life was extinct. Dr. Holyoke was at hand to receive the body as soon as it was drawn from the water and to restore life, if possible.

Had it been a case of drowning, life could have been restored, but as it was nothing could be done. The diver's death must have been instantaneous. As the air-hose parted, the effect was as if he had been struck by a terrific blow all over his body. The blood was forced out of his ears. When his brass armour was removed his clothing was found to be perfectly dry. There was no water in the helmet or elsewhere in the armour.

Constine was about 30 or 35 years of age, a strong man, five feet 10 or 11 inches in height. He had a wife and two children at his home in East Boston. Medical Examiner Tuttle viewed the body and may conclude to have an inquest of investigation.

Holyoke Daily Transcript
July 17, 1885

Another Diver Drowned

Thomas W. Conklin, a diver employed at the dam, was drowned this morning at 10 o'clock. Mr. Conklin resided in New York, was 60 years of age and had been a diver for 40 years. He was not drowned in the manner of George Constine, for at the point of the dam, where those repairs are being made, the work is going on superbly. About the middle of the dam, however, a crib has been sunk to enable men to work in it upon the dam's rise.

The two divers went down on the exterior of the crib to examine the vicinity. Mr. Conklin was drawn into a hole in the dam and it was impossible to get him out. The other diver went down again to help the rescue but found himself being drawn into the same hole and had to signal to be drawn up. Mr. Conklin's body has not yet been recovered, but can be by the sinking of a crib over the spot.

This is the Transcript-Telegram's weekly historical and literary column. We welcome reader participation.

a former vice president of the St. Jerome's Temperance Society, a local self-improvement organization that was popular among skilled Irish workers. None of this mattered in the bitter exchange that followed.

Apart from disagreements over economic matters, Lynch was particularly incensed by the "arbitrary spirit of the men." As a self-made contractor and civic leader in Irish Holyoke, he apparently expected

Italian Laborers in Massachusetts

Approximately 35 million immigrants entered the United States between 1820 and 1924, including 4 million Italians. They came largely from southern Italy, where an increasing population strained already meager resources. It became common practice for construction managers in Massachusetts and other states to hire labor agents (or *padroni*) to provide labor gangs for projects such as digging, laying railroad tracks, and supplying builders with materials. The *padrone* received a fee for each laborer he provided, and the laborer was provided with a steady income and a place to live in exchange for his labor.

The *padrone* would provide housing, food, medical care, transportation, and, at times, liquor, charging most of the laborer's wages. In many cases, the accommodations provided by the *padrone* were inadequate and sometimes nonexistent. After spending several months in backbreaking, dangerous work, the laborer would often be in debt to the *padrone*. These conditions led to sudden strikes, causing disruptions in various commercial construction ventures. For example, in the 1890s, on the construction of the Wachusett water project near Clinton, Italian laborers struck six times during the first four years of work.

By 1900, there were approximately three thousand Italian laborers in Boston and some seven thousand in Massachusetts. Over the next few years, thousands more arrived in the Commonwealth in search of work. In 1904, a few Italian workers joined the building trades unions, but the vast majority of Italians on job sites remained unorganized and in bondage to the *padroni*.

The Italian consul in Boston, Baron Gustavo Tosti, believed the only way that Italian laborers could erase the stigma of "cheap labor" that attached to them would be to organize their own union. An immigrant banker from Boston's North End named Domenic D'Alessandro became a close ally of Tosti. D'Alessandro used his organizing talents to create the Italian Laborers Union (ILU) in April 1904, which became a key weapon in the attack on the *padroni* system. With the help of the Italian consul and the American Federation of Labor, the ILU in Massachusetts eventually encouraged the enactment of laws that put many *padroni* out of business and alleviated many injustices experienced by Italian immigrants.

Eventually, D'Alessandro joined forces with the Irish hodcarriers' locals and proved that unskilled laborers could also use the craft-union model of organization. Domenic D'Alessandro won acceptance of his union by the Boston Building Trades Council and affiliated with the new national Hod Carriers' Union. In 1908, he became the International's president, a post he held unchallenged until 1941.

a certain deference from his less prosperous countrymen that he no longer received.

Although this dispute was resolved short of a strike, others ended much differently. Four years later, in 1892, Holyoke carpenters sought $2.25 for a nine-hour day and employer assurances that they would hire only union labor. Contractors had no intention of granting unionists a closed shop and flatly rejected the carpenters' demands. They also formed a builder's association, which obtained promises from local businesspeople that members would not be held responsible for unmet contracts in the event of a work stoppage.

The ensuing struggle furnished vivid evidence of the extent to which worker solidarity had become an integral feature of Holyoke trade unionism. The recently organized Central Labor Union, along with a host of individual unions, promptly announced their support of the carpenters. The painters declared that they would not work beside nonunion carpenters. The bricklayers petitioned their International for authority to take similar action. The molders sought permission from their International to decline work on castings ordered by members of the builders' association; and the printers levied weekly assessments on behalf of the strikers. In late May, the brick masons, mason tenders, and plumbers threatened to join the carpenters if an agreement was not quickly reached. This show of solidarity doubtless influenced the compromise settlement that ended the strike a month later.

As historian David Montgomery has written, the building industry provided a setting for the interaction of two major developments in Irish-American history: "One is the much celebrated rise of immigrants from rags to riches. The other is the much ignored forging of a working-class ethical code, which exalted mutuality over acquisitive individualism and promoted the group welfare in preference to individual success."

PART IV

WOMEN WORKERS STRUGGLE FOR DIGNITY AND EQUALITY, 1902-1919

THE AMERICAN FEDERATION OF LABOR IN Massachusetts had made lasting strides in organizing the workers of the Commonwealth. The base it built would be the foundation of the labor movement for many years to come. Yet in many ways it reached the limit of craft-based unionism. While white men working in the crafts were an important constituency, the cries of a growing number of unskilled workers, women workers, and workers of color were unanswered.

Throughout the nineteenth century, women of all classes struggled against traditional beliefs about women's proper place in society. According to prevailing thought, there was a natural division of labor between men and women: men occupied and worked in the public sphere of government and commerce, while women maintained the domestic sphere of home and family. In fact, this conception had little to do with the realities of men's and women's lives.

Women had always toiled in the Commonwealth. In addition to the work in the home they had always performed, the work Massachusetts women performed on the farms was central to the agricultural economy. In the seventeenth and eighteenth centuries, there was also no sharp distinction between home and workplace. As we saw in the example of

shoe production, early industry relied on the work that women performed in their homes. With the growth of the textile industry in Massachusetts, young women and girls shouldered much of the weight of the new factory system.

Women in the Commonwealth played pivotal roles in struggling for a better life for themselves and their families. They played an important part in organizing the Commonwealth's shoe and textile industries in the years before the Civil War. The Lowell Female Reform Association grew out of such struggles in the textile industry and was the strongest force for the ten-hour day in Massachusetts. Although Massachusetts women had fought no less valiantly than men for justice in the workplace, at the turn of the century they had little to show for their efforts—either in wages and working conditions or in institutional support for their struggles.

The AFL not only opposed the entrance of women into the work force and the labor movement but was largely uninterested in organizing unskilled workers. Unskilled work did not represent the same "nobility of labor" that was so central to the ethos of the AFL. Despite their horrific working conditions, their militancy, and their desire to unionize, women workers were largely ignored by the AFL.

In the vacuum, the nation saw the emergence of an alternative model of unionism, the Industrial Workers of the World (IWW), known as the Wobblies. In direct opposition to the AFL, they rejected the factionalism of craft unionism and, echoing the Knights of Labor's "An Injury to One Is An Injury to All," envisioned "One Big Union" of all workers—white and black, men and women, native and foreign born, skilled and unskilled. The Wobblies' organizing efforts ignored the skilled male workers already represented by the AFL and instead appealed directly to women and immigrant workers who toiled in massive factories such as the ones in Lawrence, Massachusetts.

Unlike their counterparts in the AFL, the Wobblies did not view these workers as obstacles to improved labor standards. Instead, the Wobblies saw in them a dynamic force capable of creating a vital union and remaking American society. Like the Knights of Labor before them, the IWW rejected the wage system and in its place envisioned a society in which workers controlled the conditions of their labor. But in place of the Knights' focus on cooperation, the IWW substituted militant confrontation through the use of direct action.

When IWW organizers arrived in Lawrence in 1910, they found a work force ripe for organizing. Yet the women and the union faced enormous odds, including a work force that was extremely diverse ethnically. But by using a variety of innovative tactics that unified the workers, the women at Lawrence prevailed in this bitter struggle. Without question, it was a victory for the working women of Massachusetts and the nation. No longer could their interests be ignored by the labor movement. It was also a victory for immigrants and unskilled workers, who proved that they understood solidarity no less than their brothers in the AFL. And it was a victory for a

new kind of trade unionism. The industrial unionism of the IWW that proved so successful at Lawrence helped redefine the very meaning of solidarity.

In 1919, as Allied leaders gathered in Europe to shape the postwar world, successive waves of American wage workers took to the streets to force recognition of their own peacetime program. Growth in the wartime labor movement enabled working people to strike for and win higher wages and better working conditions. Between 1916 and 1919 union membership nearly doubled as a result of full employment in defense industries. Wartime labor shortages also paved the way for significant numbers of women to enter the U.S. work force and its unions. Public approval of women's contribution to the war effort gave female wage workers the confidence they needed to organize.

The first major struggle of 1919 occurred in Seattle, where a general strike led by 35,000 shipyard workers brought the city to a standstill. In other conflicts, 365,000 steelworkers turned out to challenge the open-shop policy of U.S. Steel, and an even larger number of coal miners left the mines to press for their demands. In Boston underpaid policemen deserted their posts after the city's police commissioner discharged nineteen officers for union activities. The most important struggle for women workers that year was a regional telephone operators' strike, which silenced phones in five of the six New England states.

Central to the operators' success was the assistance provided by the Women's Trade Union League (WTUL). Even before the victory at Lawrence, the AFL was under pressure to embrace women in their ranks. In 1903 a bookbinder, Mary Kenney O'Sullivan, organized the WTUL with Samuel Gompers's encouragement. While not a union itself, it drew women from many classes and persuasions in support of working women.

But the Women's Trade Union League did not develop in a vacuum. Since the Women's Rights Convention in Seneca Falls in 1848, women had been organizing for broader rights. Although the Fifteenth Amendment in 1870 gave newly freed black men the right to vote, this right was not extended to women. The Women's Trade Union League played an important role in the women's movement, bringing together middle class suffrag-ettes with working class women and the handful of women trade union leaders of the time.

The telephone operators' strike in 1919 was formative for women workers in Massachusetts and across the nation. Like their sisters in Lawrence, they claimed a victory for all working women. For the first time, women organized inside the established AFL. The telephone operators had held their own in the AFL, and in doing so began to bring working women into the center of the labor movement.

Lawrence strikers parading on Essex street on the afternoon of February 5, 1912.
They continued until the soldiers *(far left)* dispersed them.

CHAPTER 9

The Strike for Bread and Roses in Lawrence

JANUARY II, 1912, BEGAN AS JUST ANOTHER PAYDAY at the Everett Mills in Lawrence. It would not remain so for long. The state had recently enacted a law shortening the workweek from fifty-six to fifty-four hours, and workers worried that manufacturers would compensate by slashing wages. These fears were soon confirmed. Moments after the first workers anxiously opened their envelopes, the cry "Short pay!" rang out. Then, as word of the cuts spread, a group of Polish women shut off their machines and walked out. The next morning, payday at most other local plants, other workers saw their pay had been cut, too. Once in the streets, they marched from mill to mill, heaving rocks through factory windows and urging those inside to join them. The strike that developed was clearly one of the most momentous conflicts in American labor history.

Although surprised by the workers' response, employers initially felt confident that they could ride out the storm and refused to meet with the strikers. Mill owners in Lawrence had enormous resources at their command. At the time, Lawrence was the nation's leading producer of worsted goods. The mills, an imposing chain of huge, multistoried buildings densely packed along the Merrimack, provided employment to more than thirty thousand workers. As one observer remarked, "The mills are Lawrence and you cannot escape them."

Lawrence was also the "Immigrant City." Beginning in the 1880s, a massive flood of "new" immigrants poured into the United States from eastern and southern Europe. Many found their way to Lawrence, where the population nearly doubled between 1890 and 1910 to more than eighty-six thousand. In 1912, the city had a substantial population of Italians, Poles, Lithuanians, Armenians, and other recent arrivals, who mixed uneasily with the Irish, British, and Germans who had immigrated earlier. Almost half the population of Lawrence was foreign born, more than in any other Massachusetts city.

As the city's population skyrocketed after 1890, housing deteriorated, health standards declined, and the death rate soared. In what remains a familiar response to such developments, many blamed the newcomers, even though the recent immigrants suffered most acutely. Ethnic stereotypes also flooded onto the shop floors of local mills. Interviewed by the U.S. Immigration Commission, one established worker remarked: "The little jests that break the monotony of millwork are impossible when a 'Dago' is working next to you; if you joke him, he will stick a knife into you." Aware of these divisions, overseers avoided mixing the two groups in workrooms where they depended on the experience of veteran workers, because, as one supervisor observed, employing newer immigrants in a department "would mean hiring only [new] immigrants." Thus ethnic relations in Lawrence came to be characterized by a degree of bitterness that was exceptional even for that intolerant era.

Even union leaders fell victim to this kind of

thinking. "I am willing that they should all come," William Rae of the Lawrence Central Labor Union said in an 1898 statement about the new immigration, but only "if they should live in a good respectable manner." Rae believed the presence of the new immigrants exerted downward pressure on local wage levels.

Economic differences exacerbated these cultural tensions. Wage data compiled by the U.S. Immigration Commission dramatically showed the disparity between immigrants who had come earlier and more recent immigrants. As a consequence, workers from older immigrant groups were better able than new immigrants to provide for their families. Their considerably higher wages also gave them a different attitude toward the strikes. Where even the smallest cut in pay could be catastrophic for the newcomers, established workers had more of a cushion.

Table 9-1. Average Weekly Earnings by Ethnic Group

Old immigrants (employees more than 18 years of age)

Place of birth	Males	Females
Britain	$11.39	8.39
Germany	11.17	9.53
Ireland	10.21	8.24
Scotland	11.42	9.06

New immigrants (employees more than 18 years of age)

Armenia	7.46	—
Northern Italy	7.35	6.77
Southern Italy	6.84	6.39
Lithuania	7.82	7.14
Russia	9.07	7.24
Syria	7.33	6.73

Source: U.S. Immigration Commission, *Immigrants in Industry* (1911), p. 757.

In this context of ethnic division, it was no surprise that Lawrence manufacturers believed their workers incapable of sustaining a strike. As the walk-out progressed, however, their optimism became increasingly harder to maintain. During the first week, more than fourteen thousand workers walked out. Another nine thousand joined them in the weeks that followed. Nor was there any indication that they would be returning anytime soon. "We are a new people," one striker declared. "We have hope. We never will stand again what we stood before."

Employer confidence ebbed, turning first to dismay and then to anger. The main targets of their wrath were officials of the Industrial Workers of the World (IWW), the organization that had assumed leadership of the strike. As a revolutionary union, committed to the mobilization of America's most exploited workers, the IWW viewed Lawrence's immigrant masses in a much different light than mainline unionists such as William Rae did. To the Wobblies, newer immigrants were not an obstacle to improved labor standards but a dynamic force capable of creating a new society in which workers controlled the conditions of their labor. Although the union's Lawrence campaign had started slowly, organizers gradually made inroads among local workers. During the summer of 1911, they staged a series of slowdowns in selected mills as part of an effort to moderate the pace of work and increase wages. By the following January, they were well positioned to play a prominent role in the strike.

Without the Wobblies' radicalism, most employers believed the newer immigrants would be incapable of organizing on their own behalf. Getting rid of these "outside agitators" should therefore be the surest way to restore industrial peace. In actuality, the situation was not that simple. To be sure, IWW officials made significant contributions during the walkout. They coordinated worker activities by establishing unified strike committees, and they raised the funds needed to feed twenty-three thousand strikers and their families. Without this assistance, the strike might well have collapsed earlier.

At the same time, though, Lawrence immigrants needed no instruction in the value of organization. For one thing, many local Italians, Lithuanians, and Franco-Belgians were bearers of political traditions every bit as radical as those of the Wobblies, and they provided their share of able leaders during the strike. The conditions of their daily lives made a more compelling case for organization than the most gifted orator could hope to fashion. Inside local factories, incessant speedups made work dangerous and unbearable. When workers complained, they were invariably told: "If you don't like it, get out."

Immigrants were also concerned about their children, most of whom entered the mills at age fourteen out of necessity. Testifying at a congressional hearing

Giving shoes to the children of Lawrence strikers.

Children of the strikers of Lawrence being fed upon their arrival at the Labor Temple in New York City.

about why he left school so early, one local youth said: "I would have kept on, but we did not have anything to eat, and so I had to go to work." When another young man was asked his opinion of a law that would require children to remain in school until they were sixteen, he replied that, yes, it was a fine idea: "but what would we eat if I go to school? We should live on bread and water all the time."

Camella Teoli was a young Italian girl who worked in the spinning department of the Washington Woolen Mill. Not long after she started, one of her co-workers told congressional investigators, "The machinery was speeded up and was running with such speed that her hair was caught and her scalp was cut by the machine." Although this had occurred two years earlier and she was still being treated by a doctor, Camella continued to work "because the family consists of seven and she is the oldest." Adding insult to injury, her parents had "no money to have a trial with the company" and were thus unable to contest the injury. No one had to tell the Teolis, or the numerous other families that experienced similar tragedies, about the importance of organizing.

The challenge strike leaders faced was to transform this indignation into a sense of solidarity that embraced the city's diverse ethnic groups. "There is no foreigner here except the capitalists," Wobbly orator Big Bill Haywood told Lawrence workers. "Do not let them divide you by sex, color, creed, or nationality." Existing immigrant organizations also played an important role. Ethnic clubs such as Chabis Hall, the Portuguese center, and the Franco-Belgian Cooperative furnished safe sites for strike meetings, and the relief work conducted by these

and other immigrant societies helped sustain workers throughout the struggle.

In the end, no group did more to forge a sense of unity among strikers than the city's immigrant women. They did so by continuing practices that had long been an important part of their daily lives. Where male clubs restricted membership to people of a given nationality, most women found companionship in neighborhood networks whose activities transcended ethnic identity. It did not matter whether one was from Italy, Armenia, or Lithuania.

These differences were also forgotten when they organized broader actions such as boycotting local merchants who overpriced goods or confronting school administrators about policies that disadvantaged their children. Without this foundation on which to build, Wobbly efforts to create interethnic solidarity would have floundered. As Bill Haywood later wrote, "The women won the strike."

During the walkout, women's contributions were not confined to neighborhood-based activities. On picket lines, female militancy often matched or sur-

Two Songs from Lawrence

The IWW was well known for writing topical songs to popular tunes and traditional hymns. "In the Good Old Picket Line" is an excellent example of this kind of songwriting. But the most famous song from the Lawrence strike is James Oppenheim's "Bread and Roses." It has been put to several different tunes and remains a popular labor song today.

In the Good Old Picket Line

Lawrence Strike Song
(To the tune of "In the Good Old Summertime")

In the good old picket line, in the good old picket line,
The workers are from every place, from nearly every clime,
The Greeks and Poles are out so strong, and the Germans all the time,
But we want to see more Irish in the good old picket line.

In the good old picket line, in the good old picket line,
We'll put Mr. Lowe in overalls and swear off drinking wine,
Then Gurley Flynn will be the boss, Oh Gee, won't that be fine,
The strikers will wear diamonds in the good old picket line.

passed that of male strikers. They were particularly formidable scab hunters, patrolling plant gates, searching suspected strikebreakers for lunch pails, and making life miserable for anyone who broke ranks. As local authorities learned, they were not easily intimidated. In his autobiography, Bill Haywood recalled an incident in which a group of women avenged an assault by company hirelings: "One cold morning, after the strikers had been drenched on the bridge with the fire hose of the mills, the women caught a policeman in the middle of the bridge and stripped off his uniform, pants and all. They were about to throw him in the icy river, when other policemen rushed in and saved him from a chilly ducking." To some observers, women appeared to be the main force behind the strike. "They're everywhere," one public official moaned, "and it seems to be getting worse and worse all the time."

One of the banners carried in many of the picket lines and parades read, "Give us Bread and give us Roses." The women wanted wages enough to help

Bread and Roses

James Oppenheim

As we come marching, marching in the beauty of the day,
A million darkened kitchens, a thousand mill lofts gray,
Are touched with all the radiance that a sudden sun discloses,
For the people hear us singing: "Bread and roses! Bread and roses!"

As we come marching, marching, we battle too for men,
For they are women's children, and we mother them again,
Our lives shall not be sweated from birth until life closes;
Hearts starve as well as bodies; give us bread, but give us roses!

As we come marching, marching, unnumbered women dead
Go crying through our singing their ancient cry for bread.
Small art and love and beauty their drudging spirits knew.
Yes, it is bread we fight for—but we fight for roses, too.

As we come marching, marching, we bring the greater days.
The rising of the women means the rising of the race.
No more the drudge and idler—ten that toil where one reposes.
But a sharing of life's glories: Bread and roses! Bread and roses!

Camella Teoli

After her injury in the Washington Mill, Camella Teoli was one of several teenage workers who testified during hearings on the strike in Lawrence, Massachusetts, held from March 2 through March 7, 1912, in the 2nd session of the 62nd Congress.

Statement of Camella Teoli

THE CHAIRMAN. Now, did you ever get hurt in the mill?

MISS TEOLI. Yes.

THE CHAIRMAN. Can you tell the committee about that—how it happened and what it was?

MISS TEOLI. Yes.

THE CHAIRMAN. Tell us about it now, in your own way.

MISS TEOLI. Well, I used to go to school, and then a man came up to my house and asked my father why I didn't go to work, so my father says I don't know whether she's 13 or 14 years old. So, the man say you give me $4 and I will make the papers come from the old country saying you are 14. So, my father gave him the $4, and in one month came the papers that I was 14. I went to work, and about two weeks got hurt in my head.

THE CHAIRMAN. Now, how did you get hurt, and where were you hurt in the head; explain that to the committee?

MISS TEOLI. I got hurt in Washington.

THE CHAIRMAN. In the Washington Mill?

MISS TEOLI. Yes, sir.

THE CHAIRMAN. What part of your head?

MISS TEOLI. My head.

THE CHAIRMAN. Well, how were you hurt?

MISS TEOLI. The machine pulled the scalp off.

THE CHAIRMAN. The machine pulled your scalp off?

MISS TEOLI. Yes, sir.

THE CHAIRMAN. How long ago was that?

MISS TEOLI. A year ago, or about a year ago.

THE CHAIRMAN. Were you in the hospital after that?

MISS TEOLI. I was in the hospital seven months.

THE CHAIRMAN. Seven months?

MISS TEOLI. Yes.

THE CHAIRMAN. Did the company pay your bills while you were in the hospital?

MISS TEOLI. Yes, sir.

THE CHAIRMAN. The company took care of you?

MISS TEOLI. The company only paid my bills; they didn't give me anything else.

THE CHAIRMAN. They only paid your hospital bills; they did not give you any pay?

MISS TEOLI. No, sir.

THE CHAIRMAN. But paid the doctors' bills and hospital fees?

MISS TEOLI. Yes, sir.

MR. LENROOT. They did not pay your wages?

MISS TEOLI. No, sir.

THE CHAIRMAN. Did they arrest your father for having sent you to work for 14?

MISS TEOLI. Yes, sir.

THE CHAIRMAN. What did they do with him after they arrested him?

MISS TEOLI. My father told this about the man he gave $4 to, and then they put him on again.

THE CHAIRMAN. Are you still being treated by the doctors for the scalp wound?

MISS TEOLI. Yes, sir.

THE CHAIRMAN. How much longer do they tell you you will have to be treated?

MISS TEOLI. They don't know.

THE CHAIRMAN. They do not know.

MISS TEOLI. No.

THE CHAIRMAN. Are you working now?

MISS TEOLI. Yes, sir.

THE CHAIRMAN. How much are you getting?

MISS TEOLI. $6.55

THE CHAIRMAN. Are you working in the same place where you were before you were hurt?

MISS TEOLI. No.

THE CHAIRMAN. In another mill?

MISS TEOLI. Yes.

THE CHAIRMAN. What mill?

MISS TEOLI. The Wood Mill.

THE CHAIRMAN. The what?

MISS TEOLI. The Wood Mill.

THE CHAIRMAN. Were you down at the station on Saturday, the 24th of February?

MISS TEOLI. I work in a town in Massachusetts, and I don't know nothing about that.

THE CHAIRMAN. You do not know anything about that?

MISS TEOLI. No, sir.

THE CHAIRMAN. How long did you go to school?

MISS TEOLI. I left when I was in the sixth grade.

THE CHAIRMAN. You left when you were in the sixth grade?

MISS TEOLI. Yes, sir.

THE CHAIRMAN. And you have been working ever since, except while you were in the hospital?

MISS TEOLI. Yes, sir.

Maria Tomacchio, an Italian immigrant, was fifteen years old when this photograph was taken in the spinning room of the Ayer mill in Lawrence.

feed their families, but they wanted more than bread. They also wanted dignity and respect, the roses. The banner inspired poems and later the song "Bread and Roses," and the strike at Lawrence is known as the "Bread and Roses Strike."

In late January, Lawrence workers adopted the European practice of sending children to families out of town. This allowed the strikers to conserve dwindling food supplies. But the sight of young children departing for distant cities generated an enormous amount of publicity. As popular sympathy for both strikers and children mounted, local

Becoming Saleswomen at Filene's

At the turn of the century the department store became an important American institution shaping a growing culture of consumption among the middle and upper classes. It also became an important public space for both the women who shopped there and those who worked there. During this time, the sales floor at Filene's in Boston was the site of a struggle where working-class saleswomen asserted their dignity as women and as workers.

Male managers believed that women made ideal salespeople. They saw them as nurturing, familiar with clothing and all things domestic, but also good at manipulating others and making sales. Working-class women were recruited because their labor was inexpensive. However, to improve their rapport with a bourgeois clientele, they had to be socialized into the genteel world of middle-class respectability. This included instruction in speech, etiquette, and dress, as well as training in "selling skills."

The working-class women who worked at Filene's department store internalized this respectability. Although sales, like waitressing, was somewhat tainted by the public nature of the work, it was seen as much more respectable than waitressing because the public exposure was limited to bourgeois women shoppers. Most of the women working as Filene's sales clerks considered themselves part of a white-collar elite, despite the fact that they made significantly lower wages than their counterparts working as waitresses or in factories.

But this "aura of respectability" masked the fact that management's day-to-day treatment of the sales clerks showed anything but respect. The clerks were forced to stand all day at their posts with no opportunity to rest their feet. They were prohibited from using the main entrances and were instructed to use employee elevators. The saleswomen not only refused to comply but brought their irritation to the sales floor, openly discussing the issues with the clientele. Having been convinced that selling was dignified work, they resisted being treated like servants.

The dress code was another battleground for saleswomen at Filene's. Sales clerks were expected to dress for work in middle-class clothes that had to be purchased on a very limited working-class salary. The gentility of their clothes contributed to the status of their work, but also created tension as it significantly cut into their take-home income.

In 1902 the company decided that all of the saleswomen should dress in black, again at their own expense. The women resisted this requirement not only because of the cost, but also because they saw it as the establishment of a uniform or a "badge of service." By the 1920s the requirement to wear black was dropped, but the battle over the dress code continued with women being sent home and docked pay for such improprieties as sleeveless dresses and sheer blouses.

Despite these issues, there was little interest in unionization among the Filene's sales clerks before the 1930s. This was partly because they saw themselves as members of a white-collar elite, outside the realm of unionization. Filene's also worked to ensure their nonunion status through a mix of company benefits and social programs, supervisor monitoring of union activity, and company training programs to control and maintain the loyalty of the sales work force. Those who displayed union sympathies were summarily discharged, providing a clear example to those left behind.

HARPER'S WEEKLY

A JOURNAL OF CIVILIZATION

VOL. LVI.   New York, February 10, 1912   No. 2877

MARTIAL LAW IN NEW ENGLAND

Disorders in Lawrence, Massachusetts, created by striking mill-hands, resulted in the occupation of the city last week by the military forces of the State. The strikers carried American flags in the belief that the troops would not fire upon them when thus protected. The arrest of the strikers' leader was followed by the murder of four strike-breakers in a tenement on the night of February 2. The photograph shows troops protecting a mill entrance

manufacturers decided to halt the exodus. On February 24, club-wielding policemen roughly handled a group of mothers and children as the latter were attempting to board a train for Philadelphia at the Lawrence railroad station.

For the mill owners, the incident was a public-relations disaster. Newspapers and magazines subjected them to scathing criticism. Massachusetts governor Foss ordered an investigation of police actions and Congress initiated hearings on the strike. Meanwhile, back in Lawrence, there was growing concern among manufacturers that they would not be able to fill spring orders. With time running out and their options narrowing, mill owners finally came to terms with the IWW.

It was an exhilarating moment. The 1912 strike changed the way newer immigrants were perceived—both by employers and by mainstream union leaders. The interethnic unity they had maintained for nine long weeks was a remarkable achievement. As one poststrike assessment put it: "The fact of eighteen diverse nationalities among the workers in one mill has been, for the first time, shown to be no barrier to a perfect solidarity of brotherhood in a common cause." It would not be the last time. The children of these newer immigrants would be in the front ranks of the great organizing campaigns of the 1930s, not only in Massachusetts but throughout industrial America.

CHAPTER 10

The Women's Trade Union League and the Telephone Operators

Dᴜʀɪɴɢ Wᴏʀʟᴅ Wᴀʀ I, ꜰᴇᴅᴇʀᴀʟ ᴀᴜᴛʜᴏʀɪᴛɪᴇꜱ had placed telephone communications under the direction of Postmaster General Albert S. Burleson. After the war, when operators sought a new contract, Burleson refused to discuss such questions himself and ignored requests that he turn negotiations over to the phone companies. This continued for almost six months before New England operators, led by Boston's Local 1A, decided to take matters into their own hands. On April 15, 1919, telephone operators from northern Vermont to Cape Cod laid down their headsets and went on strike for a new contract, setting up picket lines outside regional exchanges.

Although the operators' organization was only seven years old at the time, it had come a long way. The union began in 1912 to fight the low pay and oppressive working conditions that workers faced.

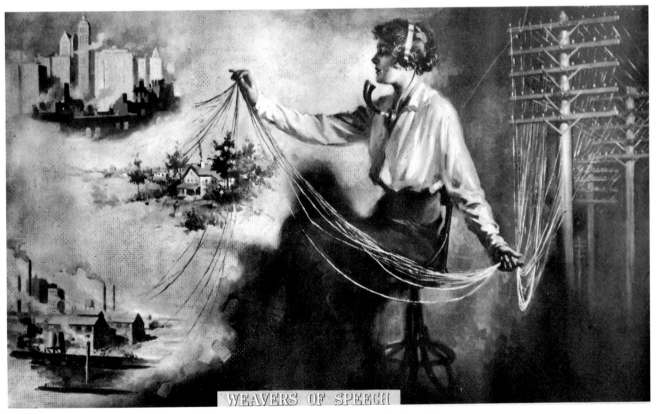

WEAVERS OF SPEECH

A highly stylized image of telephone operators used by the New England Telephone Company.

One major grievance was the "split trick," a staffing procedure that extended the workday by dividing it into two separate shifts, leaving several hours of unpaid time in between. The system placed an intolerable burden on operators. As Mary Quinn of Springfield explained: "You had no life of your own because you had three hours off in the afternoon— if you had to go home you'd no more than get home than you had to come back." Workers also objected to what a Boston operator called the phone company's "military discipline." "We couldn't whisper, we had to sit still all day. They'd fire a woman if she were five minutes late. They made her stay in a retiring room all day, until she lost her pay. They punished us. So, it was important to have a union."

Though operators wanted to organize, they knew little about trade unionism and worked in an occupation with no history of organizing. They would soon develop labor traditions of their own, in large part because of the assistance they received from the

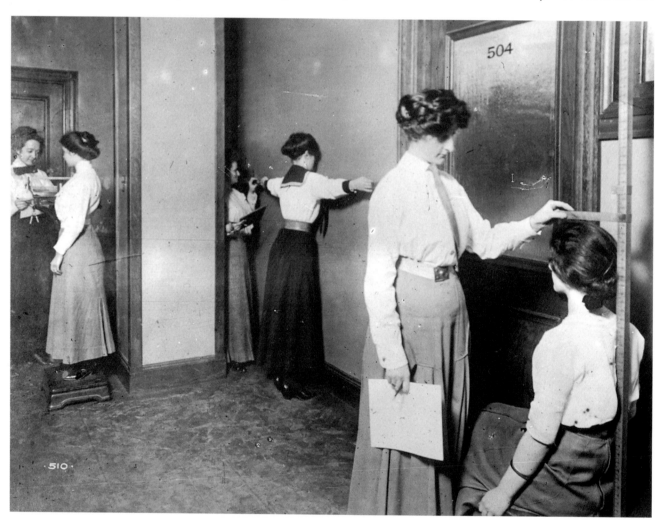

Reflecting the military discipline and cramped working conditions, applicants for positions at the New England Telephone Company are weighed and measured for sitting height and reach.

Boston chapter of the Women's Trade Union League (WTUL). On November 14, 1903, Mary Kenney O'Sullivan, who lived and organized in Boston, won Sam Gompers's approval for the founding of a women's labor organization within the AFL. That night, at Boston's historic Faneuil Hall, women from various craft unions met with middle-class and elite reform leaders to found the WTUL. Soon there would be large chapters in Boston, Chicago, and New York.

The WTUL had its roots in the experiences of working women such as Mary Kenney O'Sullivan and in the settlement house movement founded by Jane Addams. Urban settlement houses provided immigrant women and their families with services and educational programs designed to improve their new lives in America. Settlement houses attracted reform-minded women from the middle and upper classes and exposed them to the concerns of wage-earning women. In Boston and elsewhere, women took advantage of their contacts in the labor movement and in reform circles to build the WTUL. Soon well-heeled reformers provided essential funding for organizing activities.

The WTUL committed itself to organizing women workers who lacked union representation. It also sponsored a variety of activities to improve working conditions for women and prepare them for union leadership. As a result, the WTUL was in the forefront of campaigns for protective legislation and founded some of the nation's first worker education programs. Key demands of the League included reduced hours and equal pay for equal work. Working women appreciated the WTUL's efforts on their behalf, and, unlike male-dominated labor organizations, the WTUL valued working women's contributions in the workplace, at home, and in their communities.

The Boston telephone operators approached the local WTUL chapter for advice. League officers, including Mabel Gillespie, concluded that the operators should affiliate with the AFL's International Brotherhood of Electrical Workers (IBEW), which represented craftsmen employed by telephone companies. The IBEW quickly dispatched its general organizer, Peter Linehan, from New York. Linehan worked closely with Gillespie and the Boston WTUL to organize operators citywide.

Organizing proceeded rapidly. By year's end, the Boston Telephone Operators' Union had 2,200 members and efforts were underway to sign up workers in Springfield and Lynn. In Springfield, Mary Quinn recalled, "The chief operator and other officials of the company would find out where we were having the meeting, and they would hide behind trees, and telephone poles, and get our names, and the next morning we'd be called up to the desk and we'd be told the advantage and disadvantage of joining a union and what would happen and what wouldn't happen. But it didn't deter any of us."

Operators did not hesitate to strike in 1919 because they had already overcome a number of formidable obstacles. Their first major challenge came in April 1913, when telephone executives refused to negotiate and began importing strikebreakers to crush a threatened walkout. But the operators now had significant support from the Boston labor movement. The WTUL had assisted the operators in the formulation of their contract demands. Other labor organizations pledged their support in the event of a strike, and the Boston Central Labor Union appointed a committee to assist operators in devising an effective strategy, including picketing the hotels in which company strikebreakers were being housed.

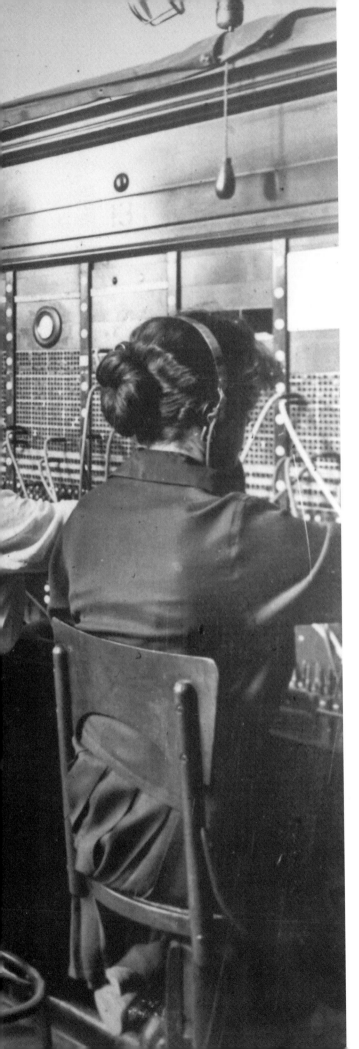

Women telephone operators on the job at New England Telephone, under the watchful eye of their supervisors (at left).

As tensions mounted, the Boston Chamber of Commerce intervened. Fearful of the impact a strike would have on local businesses, it urged telephone officials to meet with the operators and offered to serve as a mediator. Later, when rank and file operators rejected the company's first offer, Chamber leaders pressured company negotiators to reconsider their position. The final settlement increased wages and made the split trick optional for workers with more than eighteen months' service. More important, the contract gave the operators' union real legitimacy. With their Massachusetts base secure, they began organizing throughout New England and were well on their way to becoming a national union.

As the self-assurance of union leaders mounted, they became increasingly dissatisfied with their subordinate position within the councils of the IBEW. This was also the heyday of the suffrage movement, and the operators' close association with WTUL leaders had made them keenly aware of their rights as women. They challenged IBEW policies that included consigning women workers to sublocals that functioned as auxiliaries of male units and allowing women only half as many delegates at IBEW conventions as men were allowed. In 1915, they launched a "Votes for Telephone Girls" campaign that ultimately forced the International to grant them full representation and full voting rights. Three years later, the IBEW leadership created a telephone operators' department with "full authority for separate self-government."

The WTUL continued to provide assistance, primarily through its various educational activities. They were designed to give women union leaders the self-confidence and administrative skills needed to deal effectively with more experienced male managers and trade unionists. Participation in these programs provided skills that enabled union officers to do a better job of representing their members and made them ardent supporters of similar training for all women workers. As one Boston operator observed: "You never got any information about unions through schools. . . . [Y]ou had no knowledge of what you were up against." Union leaders hoped to fill that void through the promotion of workers' education. At the same time, they recognized that rank and filers had social needs, and the union, particularly after the formation of the telephone operators' department, sponsored a broad range of social activities. The overriding goal was to give operators opportunities that emphasized their dignity and self-worth as women and as trade unionists.

Battle tested and savvy, they were well prepared to confront Albert Burleson's obstructionism in 1919. They needed to be, because their male counterparts in the labor movement initially refused to back them. IBEW leaders counseled against a strike, as did AFL leader Samuel Gompers, who urged operators' president Julia O'Connor to "maintain self-control and give opportunity to those who are in a position to bring about [an] honorable adjustment." At a critical April 11 meeting, they dismissed the warnings of IBEW vice president Gustave Bugniazet and decided instead to follow the lead of a woman worker who shouted, "It took the Yankee Division to lick the Kaiser. Now let the Yankee operators lick Burleson." According to a reporter who was present at the gathering: "The utterance of this operator was like a flame to gunpowder, and any thought that was entertained by the conservatives or by International officers of restraining the meeting were swept aside,

Boston Police Strike of 1919

In September 1919, striking mine and mill workers had some unlikely company when the Boston police went on strike. Police had organized in many major cities across the country with little opposition from their employers or the general public. But the autumn of 1919 was a very different time. During the preceding war years, the American people had been bombarded by government and business propaganda fanning fears of foreign radicalism and the "Bolshevik menace." As labor unrest spread across the country, the public was all too ready to believe that the country was under attack by Reds, inside and out. When their sworn protectors, the police, seemed to join this radical element, the Red Scare of 1919 was in full bloom.

Like their industrial counterparts, Boston police were frustrated with low wages and long hours, at a time when postwar inflation gave each paycheck diminishing value. Their wages were even significantly lower than the earnings of most unskilled factory workers. For this meager pay they were asked to work as many as seventy-two to ninety-eight hours a week.

Frustrated by the failure of the city administration to respond to their wage and hour demands, the local police organization, the Boston Social Club, affiliated with the AFL in August. The new police commissioner, Edwin Curtis, responded by issuing a general order stating that "a police officer

Governor Calvin Coolidge inspects the militia during the Boston police strike, 1919.

a few street gangs and young hoodlums took advantage of the absent police and began to loot, vandalize, and harass the public, the police were accused of creating a "Bolshevik nightmare" of terrifying proportions. Although the rioting and looting were quickly brought under control by the state guard, the national media outdid themselves in fanning the public's fears. Newspapers such as the *San Francisco Examiner* ran headlines declaring "POLICE STRIKE; RIOTS IN BOSTON—Gangs Range Boston Streets, Women Are Attacked, Stores Are Robbed, Shots Are Fired." President Woodrow Wilson went so far as to declare the strike "a crime against civilization."

At the suggestion of AFL president Sam Gompers, Boston police offered to return to their posts pending arbitration of the dispute that led to the strike. Not surprisingly, Commissioner Curtis refused to reinstate any of the striking police and instead proposed to replace them with an entirely new force. He was backed up in his decision by Governor Calvin Coolidge, who sent a telegram to Gompers refusing to arbitrate the dispute and declaring: "There is no right to strike against the public safety by anybody, anywhere, any time."

Not only was the Boston police strike broken, it served permanently to taint the American public's attitude about public sector strikes and gave strong ammunition to those in business and government eager to paint even the most conservative elements of the labor movement with the red brush of foreign radicalism. It also propelled Coolidge into the national spotlight, paving the way for his successful run for the U.S. presidency just a short time later.

cannot consistently belong to a union and perform his sworn duty." In the aftermath of the order, nineteen union leaders were removed from the police force for their union activity. The next day, September 9, Boston police voted 1,134 to 2 to strike.

Striking police asked for nothing more radical than the right to affiliate with the AFL. Yet, as

and not until the strike question was put and carried unanimously did the excitement in any way subside."

Although relations with the IBEW were cool throughout the strike, the operators received substantial aid from other unions. In some cases, this help went beyond customary picket-line assistance. In Springfield, Chamber of Commerce opposition to the strike prompted the metal trades council to issue a statement advising local entrepreneurs that they should consult their own best interests before adopting a similar position: "If the corner grocer, the provision man, and the hundreds of other small tradesmen that are making their living on the trade of the city's workers are using their good money to break a strike, we want to know it. We'll take care of the rest if we've got to send neighborhood delegations to every business man in town."

In most communities, broad public support for the operators made such warnings unnecessary. In Boston, sympathy was extended even by local policemen, who abandoned their traditional strike-breaking role during the walkout. Like the operators, most Boston policemen were Irish Americans. They had work-related grievances of their own, and the strike influenced their subsequent decision to form a union.

During the strike, "society women" and well-to-do college students were hired as strikebreakers. Worker feelings on the subject were perhaps best expressed by Monsignor James Cassidy of Fall River. In addition to being one of the leading Catholic progressives in New England, Cassidy possessed an acid wit, which he most often exercised in ways calculated to delight workers and outrage their enemies. In a public address denouncing the "idle rich," he recommended the "branding" of strikebreakers. "In the old days when a woman was

Striking telephone operators pose while picketing in Boston in 1919.

crooked she was branded with a scarlet letter. There ought to be another scarlet letter today, it should be 'S' instead of 'A.'"

Meanwhile, Burleson faced mounting pressure from both the media and Bay State politicians to allow direct negotiations between strikers and the New England Telephone Company. On April 20 he relented at last. The final agreement, which provided operators with a sizable wage increase and confirmed their right to bargain collectively with company officials, spurred union leaders to undertake a nationwide organizing campaign. In a year when most strikes ended disastrously, the operators' success was a major achievement. As union president Julia O'Connor observed, the victory was not simply the result of a "few days on the battle line." Rather, she added, "It had been accomplished in the patient years before, while an organization of character, strength, and of purpose was being built up."

PART V

FROM RAW DEAL TO NEW DEAL, 1920-1939

WORLD WAR I RAISED THE EXPECTATIONS of Massachusetts workers. In fighting what President Woodrow Wilson called a war "to make the world safe for democracy," working people hoped for a new day when the government would protect workers' rights. With unemployment all but eliminated by war production demands, wage earners flooded into unions and in some industries finally won the age-old demand for an eight-hour day.

Workers and their unions soon awakened from this democratic dream when faced with a brutal counter-attack from employers. The telephone operators used the government's involvement in communications to win some measure of democracy after their 1919 strike, but like other workers, they were soon under attack as well. The crushing defeat of the Boston police strike and large national strikes in steel and meatpacking dashed hopes for a new wave of industrial organizing.

In early 1920, the federal government's unconstitutional roundup of radicals, many of them labor activists, turned the democratic dream into a nightmare. Mostly foreign-born, they were branded a subversive threat to the American system as part of a growing hysteria that would sweep the nation. The IWW, which had led immigrant women to victory in Lawrence, was destroyed during the war by employer repression, vigilante raids, and federal government prosecution. IWW leaders and activists

across the nation were imprisoned, deported, and in some cases murdered. Those who survived went underground.

Despite seeming prosperity, in 1921 a depression descended, and unions faced a new assault as bankers, political leaders, industrialists, and business groups such as the American Manufacturing Association and the Chamber of Commerce launched a nationwide campaign for the open shop. Called the "American Plan," its goal was not only to break up union and closed shops but to smear unions with the taint of foreign-born radicalism. Capitalizing on the antiforeign and antiradical hysteria that grew as the depression deepened, employers repeatedly evoked "Americanism" and "patriotism" in their campaign for the open shop.

Many industries were devastated during the twenties. In Massachusetts, the state economy contracted sharply, with eighty thousand workers losing their jobs between 1926 and 1928 alone. As a result, Massachusetts unions declined along with the nation's unionized work force, which plummeted from more than 5 million in 1920 to 3.6 million in 1923. Only the Boston building trades proved resilient during the anti-union offensive of the 1920s.

Under these circumstances, AFL trade unions became more conservative, more willing to make concessions to employers, more determined to restrict foreign immigration and to limit access to their trades. The National Association for the

Advancement of Colored People sent a letter to the AFL in 1927 which stated: "Negro labor in the main is outside the ranks of organized labor, and the reason is that white labor does not want black labor."

The Women's Trade Union League gave up trying to organize female workers and settled into full-time lobbying for labor legislation. Meanwhile, the industrial unions that had adopted a more inclusive approach to organizing now faced extinction. With the exception of Boston, where the skilled trades still exerted a strong influence, the labor movement in Massachusetts was on the verge of collapse.

With American business discredited and hard times continuing, there was growing unrest among American workers. Franklin D. Roosevelt's defeat of Republican president Herbert Hoover in 1932, however, changed the direction in which the country was heading. Although FDR was ambivalent toward the labor movement, he needed union support and the support of labor's newly elected allies in Congress if his economic recovery effort was going to succeed. With employers still reeling from negative public opinion in the aftermath of the Depression, and with pro-labor candidates winning elections in state houses and Congress, American workers for the first time in decades could organize in a climate free from government hostility.

The National Industrial Recovery Act of 1933 created the National Recovery Administration (NRA) to establish minimum wages and maximum hours. As a result, many workers finally achieved the eight-hour day and saw the end of child labor in manufacturing. The NRA, and the more positive political climate it represented, stimulated a remarkable resurgence in union organizing. For the first time, Congress enacted a law that promised workers the democratic right to organize and bargain collec-

tively. Although the NRA would later be declared unconstitutional, this wave of new organizing could not be stopped. The AFL gained approximately half a million new members in 1933 and another four hundred thousand in 1934. With the passage of the National Labor Relations Act in 1935, unions across the country finally achieved legitimacy.

By this time, however, a deep rift had developed in the labor movement. The AFL unions, dominated by the crafts, insisted on organizing unskilled workers into existing trade jurisdictions. But unskilled workers in many factories rejected this approach, which seemed to carve up their strength into small pieces as workers in a single shop could be parceled out into various unions representing different occupations and trades. In addition, most of the new workers in mass-production industries could not be easily classified under the AFL's rigid craft distinctions. Few machine operators and assembly workers had gone through apprenticeship programs and even fewer held journeymen's cards, both of which were central to AFL identity.

These workers also found the AFL's conservative leaders much too timid for the challenges presented by the Great Depression and the New Deal. In 1934 alone, eighteen hundred strikes erupted involving more than 1.5 million workers. Many occurred without the support of the AFL. Riding on this wave of more militant union activity, John L. Lewis, the fiery United Mine Workers' chief, led a band of industrial unions at the 1935 AFL convention in creating a Committee on Industrial Organization. A few short years later, the CIO would be expelled from the AFL and, transforming itself into the Congress of Industrial Organizations, became a major labor federation in its own right.

Set loose to chart its own course, the CIO focused on bringing unionism to the nation's major mass-production industries. The next eighteen months were very exciting for American unions. By the spring of 1937, the United Auto Workers had brought General Motors to the bargaining table; the Steel Workers Organizing Committee had signed a contract with U.S. Steel; and the United Rubber Workers had organized most of that industry's major producers. In Massachusetts, as well as in many other states, the activism of the CIO spurred the AFL into action.

The 1930s forever changed the American labor movement. While the Knights of Labor, the IWW, and the early AFL had represented important early organizations, it was not until the 1930s that we can speak of the labor movement as a mass movement. A significant percentage of American workers became members of the CIO or the revived AFL, and for the first time unskilled production workers were fully embraced in the labor movement. And the grassroots militancy, coupled with a labor-sympathetic government, allowed for unions and labor agreements across a wide diversity of American employers.

An unemployment line in Boston during the Great Depression.

CHAPTER 11

Surviving Hard Times

Some Massachusetts workers prospered in the 1920s, and workers such as the Boston building trades leaders helped elect Republicans to office, including Governor Calvin Coolidge, who went on to a successful presidential campaign in 1924. But for workers in the state's mature industries—textiles, shoes, and clothing—the prosperous decade held great peril. And the Republican administration offered little more than pious lectures about the virtues of hard work and thrift. Workers who had gained protection during World War I with the help of the federal government increasingly found themselves under attack by their employers.

For example, the Amalgamated Clothing Workers, a rebel industrial union formed in 1914, struggled through the 1920s. In 1921, the Boston Clothing Manufacturers Association locked the union out. The scab cops who had filled the ranks of the Boston police force treated the pickets roughly. "The union had no protection," recalled strike leader Enrico Porente, "and the police were very brutal," as were the gangsters hired by the company to rough up the pickets. But the Amalgamated's unity persisted as male tailors and cutters acted in solidarity with their "sisters" who ran the sewing machines. The union survived only by striking every six months or so to fight wage cuts.

The Commonwealth's two leading industries, textiles and shoes, were in serious trouble. Many newly industrializing regions ranging from the American South to the Far East had begun the process of economic development by producing textiles, and by the mid-twenties the industry was crippled with massive overproduction. As inventories accumulated and prices declined, mills closed and jobs vanished.

In New Bedford, a 10 percent wage cut provoked a massive textile strike. More established, skilled workers were joined by recently organized immigrants mobilized into mill committees by Communists and Socialists. The strike garnered tremendous support from the community. As striker Beatrice Pacheco recalled, "Landlords cut rents until they barely met their tax and water bills. There was support for the workers because . . . no one could see how they could make ends meet with a 10 percent cut." Yet the strike lost momentum as the months passed and, after bloody police attacks, workers angrily returned to work having succeeded only in getting the wage cut reduced to 5 percent.

After the stock market crash in late October 1929, the Great Depression descended on the Commonwealth like a dark cloud. By 1930, many Massachusetts textile centers had become, in journalist Louis Adamic's apt phrase, the "tragic towns of New England." Asked to comment on the situation, United Textile Workers president Thomas McMahon told Adamic, "Lowell, Lawrence, New Bedford, Maynard, and Fall River, in Massachusetts, and most of the mill towns in the Blackstone Valley of Rhode Island, as well as Manchester, New Hampshire, are sad, sad places." According to UTW estimates, four of every ten workers were unemployed, with little prospect of obtaining work anytime soon. Worse, McMahon added, "many have been jobless for months, some for years, and large numbers of those who have jobs work only one or two days a week, earning on the average less than ten dollars a week."

In 1930, workers helped elect Boston's colorful, popular mayor, James Michael Curley, to be governor. Curley forced a Republican legislature to support unheard-of measures, including a 10 percent surcharge on taxes, a $13 million bond issue for public construction, and a limit on the use of court injunctions to break strikes. He also pushed through an extension of workmen's compensation beyond five years. AFL president William Green declared, "More progressive, constructive, liberal laws were enacted under Curley in two years than under all previous administrations in any ten-year period."

Still, little could be done to ward off the Depression's devastating effects. The state's industrial work

A labor auction on the Boston Common in 1921. The original caption for this news photo read "Something very unusual since the Civil War. The victims were unemployed and couldn't find work of any kind."

Sacco and Vanzetti

On April 15, 1920, two gunmen killed a paymaster and his guard at the Slater and Morrill shoe factory in South Braintree, Massachusetts, stealing more than fifteen thousand dollars. Police later arrested two Italian immigrants, Nicola Sacco, a shoe factory worker, and Bartolomeo Vanzetti, a fish peddler, and charged them with the murders. Both were carrying pistols, and the draft of a radical antiwar statement, in his handwriting, was found on Vanzetti. They were anarchists who had fled to Mexico during World War I to avoid the draft.

In the "Red Scare" following World War I, U.S. Attorney General Palmer ordered massive government raids against communists, anarchists, and radicals, who were accused of plotting to take the property of others through violence and sabotage. Many, such as the leaders of the IWW, were rounded up and deported.

The police, the prosecutor, and the trial judge were clearly prejudiced in the handling of the Sacco and Vanzetti case. Witnesses identified the two at the scene of the crime simply because they were Italians, despite their credible alibis. It was evident the pair often misunderstood questions put to them in English, though witnesses said the killers spoke clear English. The prosecutor handled evidence improperly. Although the men were ostensibly charged with murder, the prosecutor made them out to be traitors to the United States in cross-examination. In the end, Judge Webster Thayer appealed to the jurors'

patriotism and religious beliefs. None of the jurors was Italian.

In this wave of hysteria, Sacco and Vanzetti were quickly tried and convicted. Before his sentencing, Vanzetti declared in his own defense: "Not only am I innocent of these two crimes, not only in all my life I have never stole, never killed, never spilled blood, but I have struggled all my life, since I began to reason, to eliminate crime from the earth."

Following their conviction, Celestino Madeiros confessed to taking part in the Braintree killings as a member of a professional gang. Using this lead, the defense gathered new evidence that pointed toward the "Morelli" gang and away from Sacco and Vanzetti. Agents of the U.S. Justice Department had been watching two members of the Morelli gang, yet requests to open up their files to the defense were refused. The trial judge rejected a series of motions for a new trial based on the new evidence. Despite outpourings of support from around the world, the Massachusetts Supreme Judicial Court also refused to reopen the case. A final appeal to the governor for clemency failed, and Sacco and Vanzetti were sent to the electric chair on August 22, 1927.

Fifty years after their execution, Governor Michael Dukakis issued a proclamation stating that Sacco and Vanzetti were tried in an atmosphere "permeated by prejudice against foreigners and hostility toward unorthodox political views" and that therefore "any stigma of disgrace should forever be removed" from their names.

Demonstration protesting the conviction of Sacco and Vanzetti in the North End of Boston.

force dropped from 695,000 in 1920 to 481,000 in 1930, the largest erosion in the nation. By January 1934, a special census showed that one-quarter of the Commonwealth's work force was wholly unemployed and more than 60 percent of those people had been unemployed for at least a year.

Conditions in Lynn, Brockton, Stoneham, Haverhill, Newburyport, and other shoe towns were equally grim. As one union leader put it, they had been "cursed by the awful chaos within the shoe-manufacturing racket." Composed principally of small producers who rented their equipment from the United Shoe Machinery Company, the industry exhibited some of the worst forms of cutthroat competition. Manufacturers "get a shoe model that they think will sell," a Haverhill public official explained to Adamic, "and then they work day and night producing that model." The invariable result was overproduction, followed by widespread layoffs. "Now there's no work," this official said. "And the workers who made millions of pairs of shoes [find that they] did not make enough to have decent shoes on their own feet!"

These developments were not confined to textile and shoe workers. As unemployment mounted in these major industries, other businesses also suffered. The first to be affected were construction workers. Building activity is extremely sensitive to changes in the general economy, and as early as 1928 the jobless rate among union carpenters soared to 60 percent in particularly hard-hit locales.

Later, as the Depression spread and deepened, cities with diverse industries witnessed scenes as tragic as those found in single-industry manufacturing towns. In a 1934 letter to New Deal relief

103

Massachusetts in the Great Depression

In the depths of the Great Depression Louis Adamic traveled across the country documenting the misery of Americans for his book *My America*. This excerpt, found on pages 268 and 269 of his book, is from his stop in Massachusetts.

In Lowell I saw shabby men leaning against walls and lamp-posts, and standing on street corners singly or in twos or threes; pathetic, silent, middle-aged men in torn, frayed overcoats or even without overcoats, broken shoes on their feet (in a town manufacturing shoes!), slumped in postures of hopeless discontent, their faces sunken and their eyes shifty and bewildered—men who winced and jerked queerly when they noticed me looking at them, and shuffled off uncertainly, wringing their hands in a mingling of vague desperation and of resentment at my gaze. I spoke or tried to speak with some of them, and I went into a few of the unemployed's homes in Lowell and heard and saw things which, if I described them, would make very melancholy reading.

But even so I was scarcely prepared for the painfully awry conditions that I found in Lawrence, once the leading wool and worsted city in the United States, a half hour's trolley ride from Lowell. . . .

Lawrence, with its tremendous mills, was a "mistake," which the mill owners had been trying to rectify by operating the mills only a little more than was necessary to pay the overhead on the old mills, and thus killing the unions; for when jobless or working only part-time, workers cannot pay their union fees. The process of rectifying this "mistake" was still going on when I came. And it was a painful process to the people—especially the working people—of the city of Lawrence.

I happened to arrive before daybreak on a Monday morning and, walking about, saw hundreds of shabby, silent, hollow-eyed men and women, native and foreign born, going toward the immense, dark mills. I discovered later that very few of them were going to work; most were seeking work. On Mondays they usually went to the mills to learn from the employment managers if any help would be needed during the week. Many of them had been making these Monday-morning pilgrimages for months, some of them for years, getting only a day's or two days' work now and then.

By eight o'clock the great majority of them were returning from the mills. Some had been told to come to work on Wednesday or Thursday or Friday; others, perhaps a majority of them, were told there was no work for them this week. Perhaps next week.

Women hurried home. Men stood on curbs, wretchedness inherent in their every action and aspect; penniless men, most of them without any intelligent, objective idea of what was happening to them, what was going on in Lawrence or in the textile industry. One of them said to me, "I don't know nothing, only that I have no job. No job—no job," he repeated in a shrill, half-hysterical voice.

EXPOSED!

—Starvation Wages
—Unhealthy Surroundings
—Grinding Toil
—Crooked Shop Owners

REVEALED IN ACTUAL STORIES of GIRLS WHO WORK

in Massachusetts

Sweat Shops

Stories of shocking abuses, cruel treatment, and deplorable conditions, the truth about sweat shops, that cancerous evil eating out the lives of underpaid workers in Massachusetts.

EXCLUSIVELY in TOMORROW'S

Sunday Advertiser

Largest Sunday Circulation in New England

This advertisement appeared in the *Lowell Sun*, May 13, 1933.

administrator Harry Hopkins describing conditions in Boston, Martha Gellhorn wrote "that whatever words I use will seem hysterical and exaggerated." Inside the homes of jobless workers, she saw "fear, fear driving them into a state of semi-collapse; cracking nerves; and an overpowering terror of the future."

As hopeless as things seemed, most workers continued to search for employment. Some workers revived the time-honored tradition of tramping. "You just had to keep traveling," said one carpenter who adopted this strategy: "A hundred miles a day. Stop at a job and ask if they needed help." Countless workers shared the experience of a Pittsfield job seeker who "went from street to street, from location to location, from manufacturer to manufacturer looking for an hour's pay, four hours' pay, or a day's pay." Those who were lucky "might get three days' pay."

Forced to eliminate all but the most necessary items from family budgets, working people in Massachusetts made do as best they could. They grew their own food on plots of vacant land. They patched and mended anything that was still wearable, and they bartered goods and services with equally cash-poor neighbors. For many, this was not their first encounter with poverty. "We had nothing before and nothing now," said Sophie, a Polish immigrant who had lost her job in a Lowell mill. "Faced with starvation, we began to eat anything that was consumable. During the summer, dandelion greens were our diet. During the winter, we ate hard bread, sweetened with sugar if we were that lucky. Everywhere people starved, raiding garbage to stay alive." Often local breadlines and soup kitchens were the only recourse. This was particularly painful for newer immigrants such as Sophie, who often faced ethnic discrimination as well as long waits.

"People like us who were poor and powerless received nothing," she recalled. "Those who knew someone or the person who gave out the food always got more. It was not unusual for us to walk away empty-handed. Pity and sympathy were emotions that these officials hid. How they could knowingly refuse a person food to give it to someone else was beyond our understanding."

If the Depression sometimes brought out the worst in people, it often revealed the best. It did so in part because of the sense of shared deprivation among jobless workers. "In spite of the rough times," Sophie observed, "we had one and only one consolation—everyone was as bad off as we were." "People were good to one another in them days," Lowell's Yvonne Hoar remembered. "They shared a lot. If you didn't have something and they did, they'd give it to you. If you had neighbors and you didn't have anything to eat, they'd take you in and feed you. If they didn't have anything, well, you fed them."

CHAPTER 12

The Birth of the CIO and the Revival of the AFL

WITH THE ELECTION OF FRANKLIN D. Roosevelt, the federal government became a source of aid to distressed working people. Taking office in March 1933, during the darkest days of the Depression, Roosevelt abandoned the halting and ineffectual policies of his Republican predecessor and launched a broad-ranging reform effort called the New Deal. Federal relief initiatives, such as the

Women ship builders in Massachusetts join the CIO.

A Textile Workers/CIO organizing drive at the
Nashawena Mills in New Bedford.

Works Progress Administration (WPA), provided
many thousands with welcomed jobs. Poor administration and political favoritism marred the operation
of some projects. But such problems fade into
insignificance when compared to what was accomplished. The WPA's substantive achievements include the construction of parks, water systems,
airports, and a wide assortment of public buildings.
Many can still be seen in cities and towns of the
Commonwealth.

Roosevelt's New Deal not only made bold experiments in national economic and social planning, it
also convinced workers they had a friend in the
White House. The president appointed Frances
Perkins as Secretary of Labor to symbolize a new
approach. Born in Boston, raised in Worcester,
and educated at Mount Holyoke, Perkins shared the
social progressivism of the educated women who had
helped form the Women's Trade Union League in
1903. Like the president, she took a positive view
of government's role in a democratic society. Breaking with the past, President Roosevelt declared:
"Better the occasional faults of government that
lives in a spirit of charity than the constant omission
of a government frozen on the ice of its own
indifference."

The National Industrial Recovery Act of 1933
created a federal agency, the National Recovery
Administration (NRA), and, among other provisions, set minimum wages and a limit on working
hours. It also established, for the first time in U.S.
history, the legal right for workers to organize into
unions. As a result, unorganized workers across the
Commonwealth rushed to join AFL locals. FDR

Civilian Conservation Corps student workers, returning from work in the woods of Breakheart Camp in Saugus.

publicly announced that if he worked in a factory, he would join a union, which encouraged organizing further.

Workers adopted the strike weapon, which had fallen into disuse during the Depression. The number of industrial disputes in Massachusetts shot up from 76 in 1932 to 157 in 1933. In the most important strike of that turbulent year, five thousand leather workers walked out in Lynn, Peabody, and other towns. The tannery owners imported strikebreakers but local residents, especially ethnic organizations, supported the leather workers in their successful strike which paved the way for a national union. Even cranberry pickers struck the bogs around Wareham. Fifteen hundred field hands, mostly Cape Verdeans, struck for union recognition to raise pathetic wages and curb the harsh rule of field bosses. Although this first agricultural strike in the state's history failed, many others would succeed in the intoxicating New Deal atmosphere.

Across Massachusetts industrial workers considered unorganizable by craft unions demonstrated their militancy and solidarity. With even the limited encouragement of federal law, an explosion of militancy and organizing followed.

At General Electric's massive Lynn River works, Scottish craftsman Albert Coulthard revived the pattern–makers' union and soon sought support from less skilled workers. At Market Forge in Chelsea, a diverse work force of Polish and Italian workers formed an independent union after their employer reduced the workweek in accordance with NRA codes but also reduced wages by 20 percent. Led by Jewish socialists, the union struck and forced the company to sign an agreement on August 15, 1933.

In the spring of 1935, Congress passed the Social Security Act and a sweeping new federal labor law. Sponsored by Senator Robert Wagner and Lynn's pro-union congressman William Connery, the National Labor Relations Act (NLRA) created the National Labor Relations Board (NLRB), with real power to enforce workers' rights to organize and bargain collectively. The Wagner-Connery Act also banned company unions and prohibited "unfair labor practices" by employers. Workers' militant response to the 1933 National Recovery Act pushed Congress and the president into enacting the most sweeping social reform in the twentieth century. The Wagner Act allowed the labor movement to democratize the American workplace to a degree employers found quite horrifying. As a result of the NLRA, labor organizing surged forward again, especially after President Roosevelt won a smashing reelection campaign in the fall of 1936. Massachusetts union membership rose from only 155,342 in 1932 to 224,000 in 1936 and a labor militancy gripped the state as days lost in strikes skyrocketed.

The new industrial unions that broke from the AFL as part of the Committee on Industrial Organizing (CIO) surged forward in 1936 and 1937 when forty thousand workers joined labor organizations in the Commonwealth. Labor disputes leapt by 153 percent in Boston. CIO unions in the clothing industry fought pitched battles in the streets. Others joined the new CIO organizing committees for textile workers and steelworkers. Gas and coke workers affiliated directly with John L. Lewis's United Mine Workers District 50, so that all levels of workers could join the same organization regardless of craft. Others took their independent unions into the new CIO organization.

The pattern makers at General Electric in Lynn joined the new United Electrical and Radio Workers (UE) in 1936, as did Westinghouse and American Bosch workers in Springfield. The Market Forge workers in Chelsea affiliated with the new Steel Workers Organizing Committee. The rubber workers of East Cambridge and Chicopee went CIO, as did the packinghouse workers of Boston and Somerville.

The CIO unions made good use of the recently formed National Labor Relations Board to challenge employers' anti-union practices. Although the NLRB had come under employer attack, its constitutionality was upheld by the Supreme Court in 1937. A year later, the Court ruled against an important vestige of anti-unionism, the company union, when the employee-representation plan imposed by Bethlehem Steel in Fore River shipyards was declared illegal. Membership in the CIO's Marine and Shipbuilding Union surged at the Quincy yards and a collective bargaining agreement soon followed. At Boston Edison, where a company union prevailed, workers formed an independent union. The new brotherhood later affiliated with the CIO's Utility

A. Philip Randolph and Black Railroad Workers

Boston's black population grew after the Civil War, rising from the 3,496 counted in the 1870 census to more than 11,500 in 1900. With the influx of southern migrants, the community expanded to sections of the South End, including a neighborhood developed along Columbus Avenue near the Boston and Albany Railroad yard.

African Americans were concentrated in railroad work because they were excluded from other occupations while the Pullman Company and the railroad industry actively recruited them to serve their passengers. By the 1920s, the Pullman Company, with twelve thousand black employees, was the largest employer of black workers in the country. Black porters, however, suffered from long hours and low wages. They were paid sixty dollars a month for a work period of four hundred hours and they often worked twenty-four-hour stretches. They also resented Pullman's paternalism and would cringe to hear themselves addressed as "George" rather than by their given names.

As more black workers entered the industry, they became discontent with long hours, low wages, and racial discrimination. "In the old days there were twelve sections of upper and lower berths on each car. And just one porter to a car," reported Boston porter Lewis Wade in an interview. "So you had to do an awful lot of work in those days. That was really *hard* work."

The Brotherhood of Sleeping Car Porters was

A. Philip Randolph, civil rights leader and leader of the Sleeping Car Porters Union.

formed in New York City in August 1925 with Asa Philip Randolph as its chief organizer. The Brotherhood demanded recognition and a 240-hour work month, a basic $150 monthly wage, and "by no means least, the porters were to be treated like men."

In 1928, ten thousand porters from the Brotherhood voted to strike. When Randolph called the strike off, the Pullman Company attempted to fire those porters who had voted to walk out. In the aftermath, the Brotherhood lost most of its members, dropping from seven thousand in 1928 to seven hundred in 1932, with just three members remaining in Boston.

Despite the effects of the Great Depression, the Brotherhood prevailed. With the help of the New Deal, it was certified as the porters' official bargaining agent and in 1937 Randolph negotiated the first contract with Pullman, winning the 240-hour work month and many other improvements in porters' wages and working conditions. The contract also achieved a basic measure of humanity for porters by insisting that each one be called by his own name.

In 1963, Randolph confirmed his stature as a leader of the modern civil rights movement by organizing a march on Washington for jobs and justice. At the Lincoln Memorial, Randolph's deep voice intoned these profound words, "Let the nation know the meaning of our numbers. We are not a pressure group. We are not an organization. We are not a mob. We are the advance guard of a massive moral revolution that is not confined to the Negro, nor is it confined to civil rights, for our white allies know that they are not free while we are not."

Workers Union of America through Local 369 for maintenance and production workers and Local 387 for clerical workers.

The eruption of a socially conscious and broadly inclusive CIO movement attracted a whole new generation of union activists, including Poles, Russians, Lithuanians, Italians, Greeks, and Portuguese workers who had not found a home in AFL craft unions. Important leaders emerged from this CIO generation—people such as Joseph Salerno of the Clothing Workers, Salvatore Camelio of the Rubber Workers, Phil Kramer of the Garment Workers, and J. William Belanger of the Textile Workers. The Textile Workers also recruited James Boutselis from Lowell, Johnny Chupka from East Douglas, and, from Fall River, Michael Botelho and the Azorean soccer hero, Mariano Bishop. After leading the massive 1934 textile strike that swept Fall River and then building the CIO's Textile Workers Union, Bishop became an international vice president of his union.

African American workers expressed high hopes for the CIO, joining new unions where they had they opportunity. For example, in the battles raging in Boston's garment district, black women pressers allied with Jewish men in Local 12 of the International Ladies' Garment Workers' Union to keep employers from underpaying females. Indeed, "three progressive Negro" members headed up the effort, ILG organizer Rose Pesotta recalled. The union hired Mary Sweet to organize other black women pressers in the garment district and, despite "very discouraging" circumstances, by 1938 she had helped organize a hundred of her sisters.

The hopes of black workers for the CIO, however, were not realized because, due to racial discrimination, few African Americans found employment in the industries the CIO was organizing. Conse-

Mayor Curley adjusts the microphone for
Franklin Roosevelt.

quently, the CIO brought few black activists into
their ranks.

The CIO did organize a significant number of
women; however, few women leaders rose from the
ranks. The most prominent CIO women, Florence
Luscomb of the Office and Professional Workers and
Rose Norwood of the Garment Workers, had long-
established careers as activists, extending back to the
suffrage and socialist movements.

The CIO's efforts to organize the unorganized
threatened the old unions and the threat revived
many AFL affiliates. The Teamsters Union Local 25
exploded from a struggling band of 335 truckers in
1933 to a massive organization of 5,500 in 1940. Local
25 became the hub of a wheel that encompassed drivers and warehouse workers all over New England.
The Brotherhood of Sleeping Car Porters, which
also remained loyal to the AFL, won a contract
from the Pullman Company in 1937 and became the
first black union in the United States to achieve
national recognition.

The big surge in unionism between 1937 and
1940, when labor union membership in Massachusetts leapt to 307,250, came more through the AFL's
ranks than it did through the new unions. The
number of CIO affiliates in Massachusetts increased
from 44 in 1935 to 213 in 1940, but the new unions
had not penetrated the AFL stronghold in Boston
very deeply. Indeed, in 1939, after the famous "hot
dog strike," some of the city's packinghouse workers
voted to join the Teamsters rather than the CIO. By
1940 the AFL unions in Massachusetts exceeded the
CIO unions in membership by a significant margin.

But the CIO provided much-needed political
support for the New Deal and its state leaders, as

James Boutselis: "The Trouble-maker"

Interview with James Boutselis from Mary Blewett's *Surviving Hard Times: The Working People of Lowell.* This excerpt is found on pages 284–289.

In 1938, at the age of nineteen, I was working in the dye house at the Merrimack Manufacturing Company. The dye house is what is commonly known as the color room where the cloth is dyed after it is woven and finished upstairs. I had a partner working next to me, and we used to start work at seven in the morning. From seven till nine in the morning, you couldn't see one or two feet beyond you because of the steam that was generated as you started to work. That steam would sort of fade away around nine or ten o'clock. . . .

I got together with a friend of mine, Jimmy Angelopolis, to organize the Merrimack. He worked in the weaving end of the mill, and I worked in the finishing end. He spoke no English, didn't know how to read or write. He was a socialist in a way, like a little boy looking for the justice he couldn't find anywhere. He took it out on organizing. I became the business agent when I was twenty: the

youngest paid business agent in America.

Unions were few and far between. The plant that we worked for employed about three thousand people. I immediately set out to organize, not knowing anything about unions. I had several thousand so-called membership cards printed. The entire operation cost approximately $12 for three thousand cards. We didn't have the money. We had to pass the hat around to collect it, and once we did that we circulated the cards throughout the mill. . . .

We called mass meetings first. The people voted to enter into the strike, and for seven weeks we were picketing the company for our demands. For seven weeks nobody was receiving any pay. There were hardly any welfare benefits at the time, and the business community was against the strike. We were vilified and called Communists and radicals and everything else because we were trying to elevate the standard of living of the people. . . .

During the first seven weeks of the strike at the Merrimack, they brought in trailer loads of so-called scabs, people who meant well but didn't know the meaning of trade unionism. They were unemployed

[textile workers] and had been unemployed all those years. The company would go to New Hampshire and Vermont and bring these people in, load them in these trailer trucks, and try to bring them through the picket lines. In some cases they were successful; in other cases they were not successful. The violence was kept to a minimum because we were able to talk these people into not working and hurting those who were out picketing for a decent living.

Finally, after seven weeks, the company acceded to our demands, not because they wanted to, but because at that time Europe was [at war], and the company had orders from the War Department to produce cloth and other orders from France. And the United States Army and Navy were also contracting, and cloth was at a premium. So the government—the governments of these countries as well as the United States—was pressuring the Merrimack Manufacturing Company for production. Out of necessity they capitulated. They granted the wage increase, and we went back to work. That was my first experience with the union. The following year, we struck again and again. We had three straight strikes.

well as for President Roosevelt's 1936 reelection campaign. The CIO also lobbied aggressively for a bill cosponsored by Senator David I. Walsh and Boston Congressman Arthur Healey to require minimum labor standards on federal contracts. The Walsh-Healey Act of 1938 was the most extensive and lasting federal attempt to impose the eight-hour day—and a fitting tribute to the Massachusetts activists who began the eight-hour movement during the Civil War.

In 1937, former governor James Michael Curley seemed assured of winning another term as mayor

The Teamsters Organize the Roads

Boston played an important role in the birth of the International Brotherhood of Teamsters. A member of Boston's Local 25 of the Teamsters, Daniel J. Tobin, quickly became a recognized national leader. In 1907, when he led a strike in the city, he emerged as a compromise candidate for the presidency of the Teamsters' union when the national convention met in Boston. Teamster membership in Massachusetts grew slowly until the Great Depression, when it dropped by half. Only 3,709 members belonged to the Brotherhood in 1932.

However, in 1933 a dynamic new group of Boston Teamsters, led by John M. Sullivan, helped change Teamster policy on a local and national scale. Sullivan's progressive organizing program began to bring a large influx of new members. At his first meeting in April 1933, more than 800 workers applied for membership. Between 1933 and November 1938, each meeting of Local 25 brought in at least 35 and once as many as 600 new members.

Sullivan was so successful in negotiating for Boston Teamsters that wages and conditions for members quickly outstripped the rest of the industry in New England. Sullivan realized that conditions throughout the region had to be improved in order to ensure continuing progress in Boston. Union representatives canvassed the New England states in 1933 and 1934, organizing sixteen important new locals.

In 1935, Congress gave the Interstate Commerce Commission power to regulate the trucking industry by setting safety standards for drivers and trucks, awarding operating rights, and fixing the rates trucking firms could charge. These regulations made it easier to organize new groups of workers.

Sullivan presented Boston employers with a demand for a greatly improved contract in 1938. When rebuffed, he called the first general strike of New England Teamsters in more than thirty years. The aim was to improve wages and conditions throughout Massachusetts, Connecticut, and Rhode Island. On January 5, 1939, the union reached a compromise settlement after an eleven-day strike, but relations remained strained and a second general strike erupted in March 1939. This three-week-long strike was a great success, resulting in a uniform contract for all Teamsters in the three-state area.

of Boston. He enjoyed strong AFL support and attacked the CIO as a Communist-led movement. But Curley, "the rascal king" of Boston politics, lost in a shocking upset to his young protégé, Maurice Tobin, who had been elected to the legislature in the 1920s while working as an IBEW member in the telephone company. Tobin attacked Curley's old style of corrupt patronage politics and ran as an ardent defender of the New Deal. Mayor Tobin's reelection campaigns received strong CIO support and he later rose to national prominence as President Harry S. Truman's Secretary of Labor.

Labor-management relations were changing dramatically. For the first time, the federal government and the federal courts intervened on the side of unionized workers to protect the expansion of democracy into the workplace. The National Labor Relations Board made a tremendous difference in forcing employers to allow unions to organize and to permit a real democratic process to determine how workers would be represented in conducting their own affairs and in collective bargaining with

management. The Supreme Court even reversed a longstanding precedent of ruling against freedom of speech for organized workers by affirming the constitutional right to peaceful picketing.

Despite the differences between the AFL and the CIO, the charges and the countercharges, a new spirit encompassed the labor movement. More than eighty thousand new members were organized in Massachusetts between 1935 and 1940. Both the CIO and the AFL found new leaders, many of them the children of immigrants who displayed a new aggressiveness toward employers and made strong new demands upon government.

A great cultural change was taking place in American society. In the 1920s, the anti-union employers trumpeted their "American Plan" as a means to preserve their privilege over masses of new immigrants. Now, a working class composed mainly of immigrants and their descendants used the labor movement and the New Deal to assert its own Americanism. And as a result, their struggles helped reshape America as it emerged from the Great Depression.

PART VI

LABOR IN THE MODERN COMMONWEALTH, 1940-1955

I N THE END, IT WAS NOT NEW DEAL SOCIAL programs but participation in World War II that brought America out of the Great Depression. As government outlays soared—from $6.2 billion in 1940 to $89 billion by 1944—unemployment all but disappeared. By 1949 the number of jobless in the nation had fallen to 700,000 workers.

As workers became more secure, they also became increasingly militant, especially as they saw their employers' profits soaring while their own wages and benefits remained stagnant. In 1941 alone, there were more than 4,200 strikes, bringing labor victories at longtime anti-union strongholds such as Ford and Bethlehem Steel. To ensure a measure of stability, President Roosevelt established the National War Labor Board (NWLB) in June 1942 to oversee labor relations during the war. In exchange for a no-strike pledge from union leaders, the NWLB allowed cooperating unions to require all new hires to become members of the unions.

Once in place, this policy facilitated a dramatic surge in union strength. Nationwide, the number of workers carrying union cards leapt from 8.9 million in 1940 to 14.8 million at war's end. War production swelled the ranks of the Textile Workers Union of America from 83,000 to 301,000 and the United Electrical Workers from 39,000 to 102,000.

Unions also made advances at the bargaining table despite a federal cap on wage increases. Labor negotiators secured contracts that improved fringe benefits, recognized the seniority principle, and continued earlier efforts to establish effective grievance procedures that gave workers a mechanism to challenge changes in shop-floor conditions.

When the United States entered the Second World War in December 1941, the employment picture improved dramatically for Massachusetts workers and their unions. The state's machine shops, arsenals, shipyards, mills, and factories soon operated at full speed and in some cases around the clock. The Springfield Armory grew from a thousand employees in 1936 to fourteen thousand in 1943.

At the Armory, as in most war-based production facilities across the state, women made up a substantial part of the work force. In many ways, World War II did for women what neither the Knights of Labor, the IWW, nor the CIO could. As women gained access to jobs that for generations had been seen as exclusively men's work, a new world opened up for them. And although much of this openness quickly vanished once the war was over, the gender divide in American workplaces was changing.

World War II also presented a remarkable opportunity for the Commonwealth's employers. Yet, beginning a trend that would continue into the 1980s, many employers failed to invest profits back into their businesses. The Massachusetts textile industry is the most dramatic case in point. Despite tremendous wartime profits, the vast majority of manufacturers did little to prepare for the postwar years, failing to modernize their facilities. After the war, the textile industry almost completely collapsed, even with the best efforts of the unions to improve productivity and save jobs.

The war reinforced the standing of the labor movement as a powerful American institution, a status it had begun to acquire during the New Deal. Instrumental was labor's participation in the National War Labor Board, where trade union leaders sat across from their management counterparts, even if with still-unequal standing. With a rash of postwar strikes that demonstrated labor's militancy, the labor movement and its members emerged from the period with a newfound power.

But this newfound power was quickly checked by business and the development of the Cold War. Business had also emerged from the war stronger and more confident, having restricted union activity during the war years. Supported by a powerful business lobby, Republicans passed the Taft-Hartley Bill, an amendment to the original National Labor Relations Act. Called by UMWA president John Lewis "the first savage thrust of fascism in America," Taft-Hartley seriously undercut union rights by increasing management prerogatives and restricting the right to strike. It also included a requirement that unions sign "non-Communist affidavits," swearing that none of their staff or leaders were members of the Communist Party. Under the prodding of Senator Joseph McCarthy, a wide range of American institutions were suspected of being influenced by Communists. Just as the federal government targeted the IWW a generation earlier, the enemies of the CIO now used the threat of communism to taint union leaders and weaken their organizations.

Under increasing pressure, in 1949 the CIO expelled eleven organizations on charges of being "Communist dominated."

The CIO's social unionism was seriously undermined as the Cold War intensified. The dissenting views and progressive politics of the 1930s became very dangerous to hold in the 1950s. Stripped of much of its social activism, the CIO no longer was the radical alternative to the more conservative craft unionism of the AFL.

With the merger of the AFL and the CIO in 1955, the vision of the American labor movement was changing. Purged of its more radical affiliates and ideology, labor's focus moved from the social activism of the picket line to negotiations at the bargaining table. Bolstered by the prosperity of the post-war economy, collective bargaining became normalized and an increasing number of American workers were covered under union contracts. Disconnected from its more radical past, the labor movement was emerging as a powerful mainstream American institution.

But the legacy of the CIO's socially conscious unionism remained. This was clear in the Packinghouse Workers' struggle against the Colonial Provision Company in 1954 and 1955 in Massachusetts. It represented an inspiring example of solidarity and interracial unity in action. The merger of the AFL and the CIO actually helped win the strike, as the skilled Meatcutters supported their erstwhile rivals, the Packinghouse Workers. At the national level, the house of labor was now united into a single organization. Yet the practice of solidarity remained critical to workers and their unions across Massachusetts as they struggled for economic justice and dignity.

CHAPTER 13

Labor in the War Years

WHEN THE UNITED STATES ENTERED THE Second World War, the effects of increased federal spending were soon apparent. Among the first to benefit were the state's construction workers. Where building trades unionists had struggled desperately—and often unsuccessfully—to maintain established wage and work standards during the 1930s, the return to full employment allowed them to rebuild shattered organizations. Everywhere one looked, military contractors were crying for experienced workers, and a union card meant that workers had the necessary skills. "If you had a union book," one carpenter recalled, "all you had to do was hold it up and you'd get a job. Every foreman wanted you because it made things easy for him."

The federal government's "maintenance-of-membership clause" allowed Massachusetts unions to recruit new members without employer interference. For example, in the furniture-making center of Gardner, workers at the famous Heywood-Wakefield Company overcame years of industrial paternalism and joined the CIO's Furniture Workers Union.

The struggle to expand democracy during the New Deal continued in other ways during the war to save the world's democracies from fascism. In Lowell, women schoolteachers organized and fought an effective struggle for equal pay using the argument that a war for democracy abroad should allow for democracy at home. The state legislature enacted some equal-pay provisions supported by both the AFL and the CIO.

On a day-to-day basis, grievance procedures became standard parts of union contracts under the

Irene Lombard, a recent high school graduate *(on left)*, and Margaret Clancy, a former office worker from Dorchester, working in the war effort.

War Labor Board. For many Massachusetts workers, being able to file a grievance was a matter of simple justice. "Whoever is right—there is no more fight," Lawrence woolen worker Gabe LaDoux observed. "Sometimes the boss was not right." For others, it meant much more. Rose Diamentina, a New Bedford weaver who began working in local mills during the 1910s, recalled that overseers "used to bawl you out for things that were not your fault and you had no control over." And, however unjustifiable such harassment might have been, "You kept your mouth shut, because if you didn't, out you'd go." The development of grievance systems changed all this: "Now you can talk and send them where they came from."

As draft calls and voluntary enlistments emptied factories of male production workers, serious labor shortages quickly developed. Unprecedented num-

bers of women entered the paid labor force, many of them for the first time. Some viewed wartime employment as a way of fulfilling their patriotic duty. "I've decided that my place is at a machine where I can do something to help," said an elderly

Jeri McIntire: Woman Welder

During World War II, women were hired to fill positions previously restricted to men. As featured in Nancy Baker Wise and Christy Wise's *A Mouthful of Rivets: Women at Work in World War II* (pages 140 to 141), Caryl "Jeri" Johnson McIntire, who worked the eleven-to-seven shift at the Boston Navy Yard, describes her experiences:

To this day, I don't understand why people were telling me not to sign up for welding, as I have never regretted one minute of my experience. They seemed to think it wasn't the thing for a girl to do.

I loved it from the first day. . . . There was such satisfaction. It was a challenge. I had no idea what I was getting into but the training was very thorough and it didn't matter that I was female. . . .

In the huge building where I was assigned, the shipfitters and their helpers would lay out the steel bulkheads on the day shift so the welders could work on them during the later shifts. This was flat "on-the-deck" welding, but I liked vertical welding the best.

One sheet metal worker I worked for would lay work out for me because he was on days, and the

next morning he'd be coming in as I'd be leaving. He'd look at it, and he'd say, "I could tell a woman did this because it's got a woman's touch." There was a sort of neatness about it, I guess. Maybe because a woman sewing would be satisfied with her stitch. That's the way that I felt. It was all in the wrist.

I liked the vertical welding because it was more challenging and so rewarding to see the neat bead exposed once I removed the slag. Slag is the residue that forms over the welded bead as the welding is in progress and then you can flake it off. It can be hot. I had many burnt holes in various shirts and was glad to learn the Army and Navy stores were selling leather welding jackets.

A shipfitter's helper was killed on the day shift when a load of bulkhead steel broke loose from the overhead crane and fell on her. I often worked that area after that and always had a sense of uneasiness whenever the crane passed overhead, even though the operator would signal. All of us were really uptight that night, but we just had to keep going. . . . [We] felt that her death was terrible but the work had to get out. That schedule had to be met or that ship wouldn't be launched.

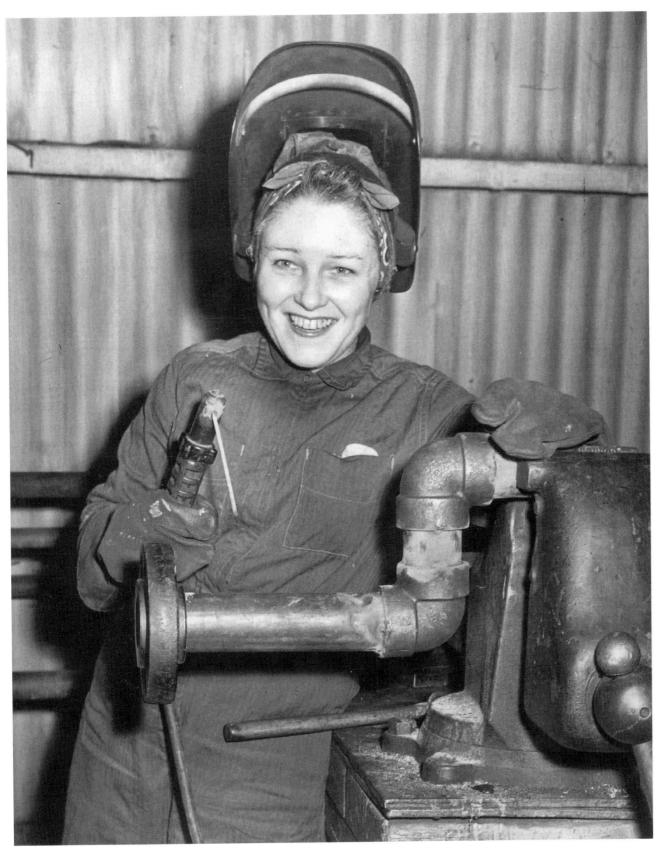

Ethel Wakefield of Dorchester working as a welder at the Bethlehem Shipyard in Quincy.

A postwar look at the machining section of Raytheon's Andover plant.

woman who had worked as a machinist during World War I and who later operated a lathe at General Electric's Pittsfield plant. "My son is missing in action somewhere in the Pacific, and I'd do anything to help now."

Others were driven by economic necessity. This was especially the case with married women whose husbands were in the service and who found that they could not support themselves and their children on what they received from the government. Lowell's Dorothy Ahearn believed that most wage-earning mothers took jobs because "they couldn't make ends meet on the allotment." Studies conducted by the Women's Bureau suggested that many single women used their pay to help support other family members as well. An examination of women workers in wartime Holyoke and Springfield showed that they spent 87 percent of their incomes on family needs.

The return to full employment with the growth of war-based industries also created new opportunities for unions. This was particularly important to workers in single-industry mill towns such as Lowell. During the war, both men and women could find alternative forms of employment in places such as Remington Arms, United States Rubber, and General Electric. "Gee, I got good money there," recalled Yvonne Hoar, who left the Merrimack Mills for Remington Arms. "I think I got a dollar seventy-five [an hour]. That was good money then." And she was not alone: "They were all flocking to Remington for the better money."

In their search for improved employment opportunities, many women experienced both geographical and economic mobility. And wherever they ended up, women frequently performed novel tasks that had long been the preserve of male wage earners. At Remington, Alice Swanton worked as a "grease monkey." "I knew nothing about machinery," she recalled. But that didn't matter: "They just handed me a pail and a couple of grease guns and showed me the machinery and they told me, 'It's a machine, put grease in it.' All the men were gone so they started using women in every job they could."

Many employers sought to limit women's gains by preserving long-standing gender divisions within the work force. They classified jobs as "male" and "female"—a common practice in most prewar workplaces—and paid women less than men. Managers tried to maintain such distinctions during the war by restricting the range of job categories open to women and by defining newly created war jobs that employed large numbers of women as "women's" work.

A few unions attacked the wage discrimination that frequently resulted from such managerial practices. The United Electrical Workers (UE), whose national president, Albert Fitzgerald, had been a winder in General Electric's Lynn plant, made equal pay for equal work a major contract demand throughout the war years. At the same time, union officials carefully monitored changes in job classification systems that expanded the realm of "women's work." Such initiatives were not only directed at women but constituted employer assaults on male workers as well. The UE made this especially clear in a 1945 NWLB case in which it contended that the "substandard wages paid to women" at General Electric and Westinghouse constituted a "real threat" to returning servicemen. "The 60,000 GE vets and 26,000 servicemen will find that many of the jobs they come back to have been changed to women's jobs at lower rates."

Women who wished to retain well-paid wartime jobs found few strong supporters outside their own ranks. At war's end, most of them shared the experience of a screw machine operator at Pittsfield's General Electric facility. She recalled, "They put the boys back on the machines. There were no women running them." The result for female wage earners was either dismissal or transfer to low-paying positions long classified as "women's work." Women who demanded seniority rights were ignored and lost union protection.

Many women willingly resumed domestic duties on a full-time basis after the war. Yet, as historian Constance McLaughlin Green found in her study of women production workers in Connecticut Valley war plants, "surprising numbers expressed their eagerness, sometimes born of necessity, to carry on if permitted." Nor was it simply "a matter of money," Green observed. "Despite fatigue and occasional exasperation over the discomforts of industrial employment, many women found in war plants a stimulating contact with a new world." After being involved in the problems of war production, "they discovered that the workaday life in machine shop and factory had an interest that neither home nor store could offer." While women's involvement in industry receded drastically after the war, these workers did not simply return to their homes. Overall, female employment increased between 1940 and 1950 as women moved into clerical, service, retail, and professional jobs to support themselves and their families.

After the war, the new postwar defense industries in Massachusetts became a battleground of the Cold War. The hard-fought election for union representation at the booming Raytheon defense plants in 1946 saw the AFL's International Brotherhood of Electrical Workers defeat the CIO. Bitter conflict erupted

An unemployed textile worker and his family describe their plight in the wave of
shutdowns in the late 1940s.

in the plants represented by the UE, especially the
Lynn works, where in 1950 the original CIO union
lost an election to a new anti-Communist rival,
the International Union of Electrical Workers. The
employer, the Department of Defense, the FBI, the
Catholic church, the CIO, and the press all called
for the defeat of the UE, which lost by the narrow
margin of 785 votes of the 11,792 cast in the Lynn and
Everett plants.

Despite overall economic prosperity, the 1950s
were lean times for the U.S. textile industry. Where

total industrial production shot up 45 percent
between 1947 and 1957, textiles registered a 2 percent
decline. The growing popularity of paper and
plastic substitutes reduced demand among industrial
users of textile goods. These developments, which
affected all textile manufacturers, had an especially
devastating impact on New England producers.
They not only had the oldest machinery in the industry, but most production took place in outmoded
facilities constructed half a century earlier. According to one industry analyst, more than 90 percent of

New England woolen and worsted factories were "as obsolete as the water clock." Such obsolescence was a major factor in the loss of nearly half of the textile jobs in New England between 1947 and 1957.

At war's end, union leaders knew that to remain competitive New England producers would have to upgrade aging plants and machinery. As Textile Workers Union of America (TWUA) research director Solomon Barkin observed, "Very few other unions in our modern industrial setup have to worry about whether the company will be resourceful enough" to secure the earnings needed to provide workers with decent living standards. In its efforts to resolve the dilemma, the TWUA urged mill owners to modernize their plants, even at the risk of eliminating jobs. At the same time, union leaders demanded that workers be given a share of the benefits resulting from increased productivity. In this way the union hoped to manage a process of industrial restructuring that it was unable to stop.

Only a handful of manufacturers, who were genuinely committed to doing business in New England, cooperated with the union. Many mills, finding that they could not continue to operate profitably, simply closed their doors. Others, hoping to slash labor costs, transferred production to nonunion southern plants. Another group of firms was only too happy to sell out to speculators who exploited special tax incentives to purchase the mills at prices favorable to both parties. These professional liquidators sometimes did little more than auction off the plant and equipment. On other occasions, they ran a mill into the ground before shutting it down.

Although the union tried to discourage these practices by urging Congress to reform corporate tax laws, they were unsuccessful. Nothing, it seemed, could halt the demise of the New England textile

industry. And during the 1950s, New Bedford, Fall River, Lawrence, and other declining textile centers began to appear annually on government lists of distressed areas. Yet, as capital fled, the TWUA did not forget those left behind. On one level, union leaders continued their efforts to aid displaced older workers, especially workers too old to obtain employment elsewhere but too young to draw Social Security benefits. After a lifetime of hard work, they faced years of almost certain destitution. The union sought to provide for them by calling for a liberalization of Social Security laws.

However helpful such initiatives may have been, they were plainly not enough at a time when mill closings destroyed the living standards of entire communities. Deeply troubled by the mounting distress that he saw in New England textile centers, union research director Solomon Barkin asked: "Where is our responsibility? What can we do for our people?" As Barkin pondered these questions, his thoughts turned increasingly to area redevelopment legislation.

Barkin proposed regional planning for economic redevelopment in the 1940s and again in 1956, with provisions for technical assistance, worker retraining, and the construction of both public and commercial facilities in distressed areas. Barkin's area redevelopment legislation represented an effort to reduce the costs of industrial restructuring for wage earners and the communities in which they lived. Despite considerable opposition, the initiative slowly moved forward and in May 1961 became one of the first measures signed by President John F. Kennedy. The final bill provided nearly $400 million in assistance to distressed areas. Of this sum, $200 million went to commercial and industrial loans, $100 million to loans for public facilities, and $75 million to grants for public facilities. Another $14.5

million was authorized for vocational training programs and subsistence payments to the displaced workers enrolled in them.

Contrary to popular myth, unions were not responsible for the disappearance of textile manufacturing in New England. Long after most manufacturers refused to modernize and left to pursue higher profits elsewhere, the unions remained. Although their efforts to keep the industry in New England proved unsuccessful, the textile unions remained committed to their New England work force. And while workers and unions in much of Massachusetts were still experiencing postwar growth in most economic sectors, the textile unions helped pioneer important social programs that would prove extremely important in the coming years.

CHAPTER 14

Boston's Packinghouse Workers

LATE IN THE MORNING OF OCTOBER 27, 1954, more than two hundred employees from Boston's Colonial Provision Company left work for a noon meeting at union headquarters. The union's contract was scheduled to end in a few days, and the workers were preparing to strike if Colonial continued to resist their demands for a new agreement. It would, as one union leader later quipped, be the "longest union meeting on record." When they returned that afternoon, they were met by local police and plant foremen, who informed them that they had lost their jobs because they had stayed at the meeting beyond a mutually agreed upon deadline. But they had returned late from meetings on a number of other occasions. What company owners really wanted was to destroy the workers' organization, Local 11 of the United Packinghouse Workers of America (UPWA).

To the locked-out workers, having to struggle for basic rights was nothing new. "Local 11 was born of strikes," field organizer John Mitchell recalled. The stiff resistance of Boston packinghouse owners had made "striking for recognition" an important organizing device during the 1930s. Afterward, unionized meatpackers often found that walkouts were necessary to force employers to negotiate wages and working conditions. This was especially the case at Colonial. According to Mitchell, company owner Sidney Rabinowitz "hated the union like poison" and never fully accepted the idea of collective bargaining. The result was a long series of work stoppages dating back to 1936.

The year 1954 was a particularly good time for the

company to mount another anti-union campaign because of the large number of jobless workers in the Boston area. They would have little trouble recruiting strikebreakers to replace locked-out workers. Senator Joseph McCarthy's Red-hunting crusade had raised fears about Communist influence in American life. It was a period when striking workers were routinely vilified as Kremlin agents and when union activists faced ongoing harassment from headline-seeking government prosecutors. Indeed, just three weeks before the lockout, Local 11's chief steward, Jim Bollen, had been called before a state commission investigating Communist subversion. Even though the hearing was, as Bollen charged, designed to "persecute militant union members," the public impression created by such media events could easily be manipulated by union-busting firms such as Colonial, whose owners often referred to their organized workers as "a bunch of reds."

As expected, Colonial immediately began hiring jobless workers to fill the meatpackers' positions. Union members attempted to keep the strikebreakers out by forming a mass picket line around plant entrances. But private guards and local police began escorting a steady flow of "scabs" through the picketing strikers.

From Colonial's perspective, everything appeared to be going according to plan. Although the strikebreakers were less efficient than the experienced meatpackers whom they replaced, the company was able to maintain adequate production—at least for the short run. Lucrative military contracts from the federal government, together with continued state purchases of Colonial products, ensured a steady cash flow. Meanwhile, support from local media sources added to the company's already substantial advantages, as union efforts to put its case before the public were severely hampered by what Jim Bollen called a "news blackout." Except for the *Boston Post*, no area newspaper would accept Local 11's advertisements.

However hard-pressed, the striking meatpackers were by no means ready to give up. Their militant picket line forced Colonial to operate with a reduced work force. The unions also instituted a "Don't Buy"

Members of the Packinghouse Workers during the Colonial strike.

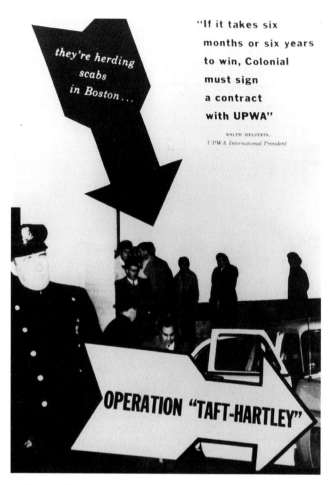

"If it takes six months or six years to win, Colonial must sign a contract with UPWA"

RALPH HELSTEIN,
UPWA International President

they're herding scabs in Boston...

OPERATION "TAFT-HARTLEY"

A flyer used during the Colonial strike linking the use of scabs and the passage of the Taft-Hartley Act.

campaign that initially centered on Boston-area retailers, who were asked to remove Colonial products from their shelves. Many willingly complied and those who did not were threatened with consumer boycotts. Later, the national union helped Local 11 expand the initiative by printing bumper stickers and dispatching organizers to stores in New York, Rhode Island, Connecticut, and New Jersey. Everywhere they went, their message was the same: "Don't Buy Colonial Scab Meat." And the more people heard it, the harder it became for Colonial to maintain its sales base. According to a union study,

six months after the work stoppage began, business had "been cut down by 40% over what it was before the strike."

Despite the news blackout, strikers also managed to reach the public because of help provided by two liberal businessmen. Norman Furman aired union commercials on his radio station, WBMS, and helped arrange a benefit concert featuring Duke Ellington that generated good publicity as well as needed funds. Cy Jacobs of Brookline rented sound trucks to Local 11 to air their "Don't Buy Colonial" appeal directly to consumers across the state. When local authorities attempted to have the trucks taken off the road, union lawyers successfully argued that such bans violated the First Amendment's free-speech provisions.

But most important were the numerous expressions of labor solidarity during the struggle. Because Local 11 had no strike fund, it is unlikely that its members could have withstood the fourteen-month ordeal without financial assistance from organized labor. The largest contributions came from the International, which furnished a thousand dollars a week for relief. Other Boston-area CIO unions also did their part, particularly those at General Electric in Lynn and Revere Sugar in Charlestown. Strikers even received support from their longtime rival, the AFL Meatcutters' Union, which forced First National Supermarkets to remove Colonial products from its stores. Initially, Teamsters Local 25 refused to respect the meatpackers' picket line during the first six months of the work stoppage. Strikers took this matter into their own hands and assembled outside Teamster headquarters one Sunday morning, distributing handbills and talking to rank-and-file truckers who were there to attend a general meeting. Later that day, Local 25 members voted unanimously to discontinue deliveries to Colonial.

One of the sound trucks used during the Colonial strike.

But company executives once again turned to the government, this time seeking refuge in the Taft-Hartley Act. Passed in June 1947, the measure bolstered managerial rights and placed sharp restrictions on union activity. One of its provisions authorized elections that allowed workers to disband their unions by majority vote. Taking advantage of this opening, Colonial petitioned the National Labor Relations Board for an election in which only the strikebreakers' votes would be counted. On March 10, 1955, Local 11 was decertified as the collective bargaining agent for Colonial workers.

Though devastating to the strikers, the company's election triumph was hardly the mortal blow that

Colonial executives had envisioned. Several days before the vote, United Packinghouse Workers president Ralph Helstein had declared: "If it takes six months or six years, Colonial will have to sign a contract with the union or go out of business." And with the exception of a few strikers who left to seek work elsewhere, the meatpackers' ranks remained intact. More important, support from the broader labor movement was greater than ever. Colonial's action confirmed their worst fears: that Taft-Hartley was a union-busting measure. What had been a small strike involving several hundred meatpackers now became a cause célèbre whose outcome had implications for unionists nationwide.

Decertification also prompted a change in tactics used by Local 11. Up to that point, intimidating strikebreakers had been the primary aim of picket-line activity. This approach was now abandoned, as union leaders decided that "only pressure from inside the plant" was likely to drive Colonial back to the bargaining table. Rank and file workers stopped harassing replacement workers and started trying to organize them. Although some union members objected, many began to meet after work at local bars, where strikebreakers often voiced their own discontent with company policies.

Through these meetings, strikers established close contact with the black employees who made up nearly half of the replacement force. Union officials believed blacks had been hired as part of a deliberate

Scabs being escorted into the rear entrance of Colonial during the strike.

The Labor Guild of Boston

The Labor Guild of the Boston Archdiocese is a membership organization of men and women committed to promoting better wages and working conditions, a spirit of fairness, and dignity for all workers. Its roots are found in the 1930s and 1940s, when the Catholic church sponsored more than one hundred "labor schools" across the industrial northern United States. These schools not only provided critical training in basic trade unionism, including grievance handling, negotiating, parliamentary procedure, labor law, and ethics, but served as a moral endorsement, a kind of "baptism" by the Catholic church, of trade unionism. The Boston Labor Guild was founded by Father Mortimer Gavin, known throughout the region as Boston's "Labor Priest."

Almost all of these church-based centers have closed, but Boston's Labor Guild continues to flourish, with 1995 marking its fiftieth anniversary. Over these decades, the Guild's membership has evolved from its original Catholic trade union base to its present composition of men and women from all religious faiths and all sectors of the labor-relations world. In addition to continued sponsorship of its adult labor school, the Guild's programs include administration of various kinds of union elections, publication of a popular guidebook on Massachusetts employment law, occasional labor-management conferences, and a speakers bureau. Beyond these specific programs, the Guild serves as a key networking resource for the region's labor-relations community, nurturing a climate of labor justice.

effort to incite racial strife. But, unlike many unions at that time, the Packinghouse Workers had an exemplary record on civil rights issues, and Local 11 was no exception. Its struggle for racial equality began in 1944, when delegates to the UPWA's Omaha convention led a successful fight to bar subsequent union gatherings in cities where hotels and other public facilities discriminated against African Americans. Later, Local 11 played a conspicuous part in equal-opportunity campaigns designed to force Boston-area employers to hire minority workers and upgrade those who had jobs.

The UPWA was also the first union that consistently elevated African Americans to leadership positions. Local 11's Shelton Coats was one example. A native of Tulsa, Oklahoma, Coats had moved to Boston in 1946, hoping to find a better racial climate. He soon discovered, however, that racial discrimination was not a uniquely southern phenomenon. It was only after he joined Local 11 that he began to feel like "part of the community." Once a member, Coats advanced quickly within the union. "I watched workers reading a book, the union contract, and I got one and read it," he recalled. "I remembered my father, who was a stone mason and a union man, reading his contract. I expressed myself and the workers liked what I said and made me a steward." The respect white workers afforded Coats, who was later elected union president, did much to relieve the suspicions that black strikebreakers had about the organization.

Another African American leader was Jimmy Johnston, who preceded Coats as Local 11's president. During the strike, he served as a liaison to Boston's black community. Johnston secured support from the NAACP, Urban League, Boston Ministerial Alliance, and two black newspapers, the *Chronicle* and the *Guardian*. In one statement, a group of prominent African Americans acknowledged the major advances "made by Negroes in the labor movement" and declared strikebreaking in a legitimate labor dispute "morally wrong." This, too, aided union efforts to sign black replacement workers, many of whom were becoming increasingly disenchanted with Colonial's labor practices.

A third black leader, International representative Donald Smith, had a particularly important role in the Colonial struggle. After taking over as strike manager in August 1955, he added members to the strike committee and got many workers involved in strike activity. Many of them became involved in the "Don't Buy" campaign, which had already cost Colonial $3.6 million in Boston-area sales alone. Under Smith's direction, the boycott became even more effective.

Meanwhile, as pressure mounted and profits disappeared, company owners began to reassess their position. The recent AFL-CIO merger destroyed any hopes they might have had of cutting a deal with the AFL Meatcutters' Union. Their options narrowing,

Colonial executives finally decided to resume negotiations. By that point, everyone recognized that there was little to be gained from continuing the struggle. As Jim Bollen observed: "Both company and union were exhausted and broke from the long battle. The possibility of ending the war was a good idea to all concerned." One major obstacle was removed when strikers agreed to rename their recertified organization Local 616, thereby enabling Sidney Rabinowitz to fulfill his pledge that he would never sign another agreement with Local 11. The final settlement was concluded in January 1956. Under its terms, nobody was to be hired until all union members who so desired had returned to work.

After more than fourteen months, the strike was over. That the meatpackers were able to survive owed much to their militancy and tenaciousness. But as important was their ability to fashion a broad-ranging labor-community coalition that embraced both old friends and onetime foes such as the AFL meatcutters. The union also received substantial support based on its long-standing commitment to racial equality. This not only facilitated efforts to attract support from civil rights groups, it also enabled the organization to make maximum use of the talents of African American unionists. After his election as union president, Shelton Coats observed that "blacks didn't have much confidence in blacks because we didn't think we had power." What he learned was "that you could get power by working in people's interests and being honest. The power I had came from blacks and whites." The same could be said for the union he represented.

PART VII

NEW WORKERS, NEW UNIONS, 1956-1980

DURING THE 1950S AND 1960S, THE LABOR movement remained strong. Offsetting the demise of the New England textile industry was the rise of the defense, plastics, and other high-technology industries. The postwar American economy was still growing at a steady pace and unemployment remained low. Despite the promise of renewed organizing by the newly merged AFL-CIO, the labor movement did not reach out to new constituencies during this period. Still, it continued to represent large numbers of workers in steel, auto, and many other basic industries. Organized labor used this membership base to become increasingly involved in political action, influencing the Democratic congressional delegation in Washington and the state legislature in Boston. By the 1960s, the Massachusetts Federation of Labor represented affiliates with more than half a million members.

However, a transformation of the American economy was beginning to take place. Although the trend was barely perceptible in the 1950s, by the 1980s it was clear that the economy was moving away from manufacturing, and significant numbers of Americans were employed in the service and public sectors. In the 1970s and 1980s, massive numbers of women and people of color entered this newly transformed economy. By 1990, they represented a new majority of the Massachusetts work force. As happened in the evolution from craft production to the factory system of the nineteenth century, the

economy was changing, and the labor movement would have to adapt or be left behind.

New federal programs, especially in the administrations of John F. Kennedy and Lyndon B. Johnson, expanded government employment vastly in areas from the Veterans Administration to the Postal Service. Massachusetts exceeded the rate of public employee growth in the nation, which exploded by 110 percent between 1947 and 1967. Public employees began demanding increased respect and pay more comparable to the private sector. A city bus driver who transported hundreds of people every day inexplicably made much less than a unionized truck driver who hauled goods.

In 1962, President John F. Kennedy issued an executive order allowing federal workers to unionize and bargain. Gradually, state governments followed this lead, with Massachusetts in the forefront. In 1958, teachers and other public employees had won the right to join the employee organizations of their choice; full collective bargaining rights were in place by 1974.

Ever since the crushing of the Boston police union and the blacklisting of its members, public employees had been reluctant to strike in Massachusetts. However, in 1966, educators in Lawrence, frustrated by school officials who refused to bargain, engaged in the state's first teachers' strike. It was part of a great wave of militancy by public unions across the nation that increased the number of strikes fivefold in 1967.

Public workers in Massachusetts and in many states around the country began organizing on all levels of state, municipal, and local government—school bus drivers, town engineers, and state mental health workers. And in the process they were changing the face of the labor movement. Not only did these union members work outside of manufacturing, they were considerably more likely to be women and people of color. By the mid-1970s and early 1980s, public sector unions became key players in the labor movement, rivaling the power of many of the industrial unions, who were already beginning to lose members.

At the same time, the American economy was shifting away from basic industry. With automation, factory shutdowns, and capital flight, the proportion of workers employed in manufacturing steadily declined. Meanwhile, employment in the service sector grew rapidly, including jobs in food service, health care, janitorial and building services, and clerical work.

Unions faced an enormous challenge in reaching out to these new workers. Women workers rarely saw female union leaders, and the union culture of construction workers, truckers, and machinists often alienated female clerical and service workers. During the 1970s, the women's movement raised the consciousness of many workers and led to more complaints about pay discrimination and disrespect in the workplace. In 1972, a new organization called Nine to Five, dedicated to recruiting women office workers, formed in Boston. Nine to Five raised important issues of pay equity, respect, dignity, and the dangers of office work, and helped spawn a new union of office workers, the Service Employees International Union (SEIU) Local 925.

Meanwhile, District 65, which later affiliated with and then became part of the United Auto Workers (UAW), began an ambitious campaign to organize office and technical workers at Boston University. This organizing drive adopted innovative tactics to counter stiff employer opposition, including a one-on-one approach to union organizing that had been used by labor in the 1930s, by the women's movement, and by other social movements including Cesar Chavez's United Farm Workers crusade. District 65's efforts at Boston University led to a remarkable victory in 1979.

Hospital workers began to organize as well. Excluded from the National Labor Relations Act until 1974, workers in Massachusetts hospitals and nursing homes engaged in little organizing activity before the 1970s. But starting in the latter part of that decade, there was a wave of health-care organizing in the Commonwealth. Hospital and nursing home workers, including nurses' aides, housekeepers, technicians, and nurses, organized in public and private hospitals from North Adams to Cape Cod.

Like their sisters at Lowell and Lawrence, and in the Boston shipyards during World War II, these women in clerical and service occupations in both the public and private sectors were expanding the vision of the labor movement in Massachusetts and beyond. They brought with them a range of new concerns and issues, sometimes including a challenge to the predominantly male leadership of the labor movement. They also brought with them a courage and commitment that the labor movement would sorely need in the hard times ahead.

CHAPTER 15

Public Employees Organize

THE LEGACY OF THE 1919 BOSTON POLICE STRIKE and its suppression created an extremely negative climate for public employees in Massachusetts. Even during the great era of union expansion from 1935 to 1955, few government workers won union protection. Federal postal workers were among the very few public sector workers who developed active unions.

In Massachusetts, public employee unionism again emerged in 1942 when Boston firefighters voted to join the International Association of Fire Fighters. With the support of Mayor Tobin and James Michael Curley, Local 718 won an eight-hour week for their members and went on to encourage unionization in fire departments across the Commonwealth.

County, state and municipal workers began affiliating with the American Federation of State, County and Municipal Employees (AFSCME) on a large scale in the 1940s. Corrections officers first affiliated with AFSCME. They were soon joined by highway employees and together the two groups formed an AFSCME state council.

Between 1948 and 1954, employees of the Department of Mental Retardation joined AFSCME chapters, and they won health-care protection in 1956. In 1953, Paul L'Antiqua organized a chapter at the Fernald State School for the Mentally Handicapped, even though he was told workers had been terminated for an earlier organizing effort. He worked with others to coordinate statewide meetings of mental health workers, which relieved some of the fear of being fired. In 1957, L'Antiqua exposed the horrendous conditions endured by patients and workers in state mental institutions.

Howard Doyle, a plumber at the Fernald School, furthered AFSCME's growth. In 1959, he worked with AFSCME to persuade the legislature to enact a grievance procedure for state workers. In 1961, Doyle became president of AFSCME Council 41 on a platform favoring collective bargaining, still seen as a radical step for public employees. At the time of President Kennedy's 1962 executive order encouraging more federal employees to seek bargaining, Massachusetts state, county, and city employees could bargain only over a narrow range of issues under Chapter 149 of the state law. Doyle pushed ahead and in 1963 he helped custodians at the University of Massachusetts form an AFSCME chapter in Amherst. Roland Messier, president of Local 1776 (so named to emphasize its pioneering role), remembered being harassed by supervisors, but with the broad support of students and townspeople the union won for campus maintenance workers what he called "the best union contract in western Massachusetts." At the same time, Ericka Pinault, who worked at Bridgewater State College, began organizing in 1963. With the help of Laura Spencer, she organized clerical workers at other state colleges and then went on to the more difficult task of organizing staff at the community colleges.

During the 1960s, AFSCME became the fastest growing union in the Commonwealth as thirty-nine new locals joined Council 41. At the same time, Council 45, composed of Boston's public workers, also gained new members. The two councils,

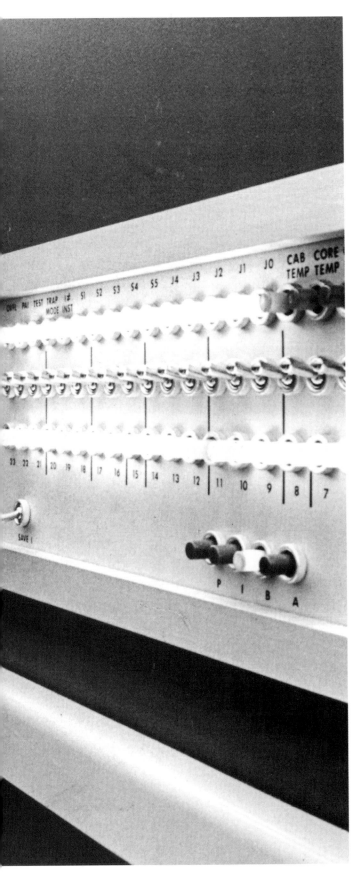

An early General Electric computer system.

together with the Service Employees International Union (SEIU), began to exert political influence on Beacon Hill, where in 1966 the legislature enacted a law allowing for bargaining on working conditions.

The previous year the Massachusetts Federation of Teachers had successfully lobbied for a new law, Chapter 763, to allow teachers to engage in bargaining on the full range of issues, including salaries. In some Massachusetts cities, poorly paid public schoolteachers joined the American Federation of Teachers. Several illegal strikes took place, including one in Lawrence in 1966. A rival organization, the Massachusetts Teachers Association, affiliated with the National Education Association, had traditionally objected to collective bargaining and union tactics such as strikes. But during the 1970s, the MTA changed and became a collective bargaining agent, representing more than sixty thousand dues-paying members, including the faculty and librarians of the University of Massachusetts, who had organized that year. As a result of collective bargaining, state salaries in higher education began to catch up with those at peer institutions, attracting better faculty and allowing the Amherst and Boston campuses to gain national recognition. MTA schoolteachers in Somerville, Franklin, Brockton, Woburn, New Bedford, Grafton, Burlington, and Fall River all struck to win contracts or contract renewals during the 1970s.

Critics of striking MTA members always ignored what the association did for students, parents, and the public education system. During the 1970s, the MTA used its formidable political power to help secure the enactment of Chapter 622, which assured students access to all educational programs, regard-

Demonstrating against budget cuts.

less of their race, gender, religion, or national origin. It also lobbied for the Transitional Bilingual Education Act, supporting education programs for students learning English as a second language, and the nationally renowned Chapter 766, which guaranteed appropriate support for a hundred thousand special-needs students.

In 1968, social workers in Boston's welfare department protested when their caseloads reached impossible levels. Led by Peace Corps veteran Paul Quirk, the welfare workers' three-day strike resulted in a victory that lowered caseloads and improved service

for recipients. In the same year, the state took over administration of welfare from the cities and towns, creating an opportunity to organize a statewide union. Along with Quirk, Rosemary Trump, Barbara Hannon, and Lynne Hollander led a march on Beacon Hill in 1969 and effectively campaigned to make SEIU Local 509 the bargaining representative for 2,200 state welfare workers. A year later, it won its first contract, allowing for upgradings and other improvements. SEIU 509 joined other public workers' unions in demanding a new labor law that would allow for bargaining over wages.

Public employees emerged from the shadows to put their case before the Commonwealth, and they began to win support. No greater testimony to the value of public employees had been rendered in the Commonwealth's history than on the night of June 17, 1972, when nine Boston firefighters died in the fiery collapse of the old Hotel Vendome. These public servants received heroes' burials, but some citizens soon forgot their sacrifice. Attempts to erect a plaque commemorating the event met with opposition from the neighborhood association in the well-to-do Back Bay, according to union leader Robert Kilduff. All this outraged *Boston Globe* columnist Mike Barnicle, who wrote "from his soul" that he had "seen more honor, pride, and commitment in firehouses and police stations and at nurses' desks in Boston City Hospital" than he had ever witnessed elsewhere in the city, including in "great universities" and "large banks."

In 1974 the legislature enacted Chapter 150E, expanding public sector unionization by recognizing state employees' right to bargain over wages. In 1975, the major public employee unions in Massachusetts began joint bargaining with the Commonwealth. The first real test of the new law came the following year with negotiation of the contract covering state

City workers picket in downtown Boston.

employees. Contract talks broke down on June 21, 1976, when the final offer by governor Michael Dukakis was rejected and thirty thousand state employees struck.

The media coverage was extremely negative and a judge quickly issued contempt citations to union leaders Howard Doyle of AFSCME and Paul Quirk of SEIU. Mediation with union leaders and state officers resulted in a proposed contract that involved concessions on both sides. But the strike had energized state workers and the membership voted to reject the compromise contract.

AFSCME's national president, Jerry Wurf, came to Boston and appointed a new bargaining committee representing an alliance of state employees. After a state fact-finding committee made a recommendation, the state employees' alliance of SEIU and AFSCME units ratified its first contract on November 19, 1976. This new agreement finally raised state workers' salaries closer to those of private sector workers, enhanced health benefits significantly, and allowed for personal, bereavement, and educational leaves, as well as other benefits.

In 1977 the two AFSCME councils merged into the new Council 93 and elected as president a public worker from the Cape Verdean community named Herbert Ollivierre, the first person of African descent to head a major public sector union in Massachusetts. A year later AFSCME negotiated a contract for clerical and maintenance workers in higher education and consolidated its gains with more than fifty thousand members.

Two years earlier the Service Employees International Union Local 285 had also expanded through a merger with the Licensed Practical Nurses Association. By 1980 SEIU Local 285's increasingly active membership had grown to ten thousand.

Public sector unions produced the first cohort of

Social workers in SEIU Local 509 protesting high case loads.

women labor leaders since the 1890s. Rose Claffey of the Lynn teachers unions spearheaded organizing and served as executive secretary of the Massachusetts Federation of Teachers from 1964 to 1975. In 1981, Celia Wcislo, Nancy Mills, and Betty Jean Andrews won office in SEIU Local 285. Laura Spencer and Ericka Pinault became the state leaders of higher education employees for AFSCME, as did Lois Balfour and Sandra Felder for human service workers in SEIU Local 509. The Massachusetts Teachers Association, representing thousands of women educators, elected three strong women leaders in Carol Doherty, Nancy Finklestein, and Roseann Bacon.

The growth of public sector unions across Massachusetts and their formation into a state alliance brought public employees into the mainstream. For the first time government workers could expect fair compensation, decent benefits, and a grievance procedure that provided a measure of dignity and respect. But public employee unions in Massachusetts also became strong advocates for the public interest. They were not only central in the efforts to improve education, but in reforms in health-care, fire protection, public safety, and environmental conservation.

We're Worth It

In fall 1984 the leadership of Local 285 of the Service Employees International Union (SEIU) began to hear grumbling from their membership about the slow pace of negotiations. Raymond Flynn had just been elected mayor of Boston, the city was in financial trouble, and Local 285's workers were divided across five contracts, with members working in city hall, the police department, and Boston City Hospital, among other locations.

Facing the difficult challenge of uniting its diverse membership, Local 285 mounted an innovative campaign to initiate bargaining, to obtain a decent contract, and to build the unity of the local. Rather than waiting for negative public opinion to cast them as greedy or self-serving, the union began a community campaign to build public support for their contract. The "We're Worth It" campaign featured a large poster of Local 285 members, the public health nurses, city hall clerical workers, parks and recreation crews, laboratory technicians, and others who provided critical services to the residents of Boston. The posters were prominently displayed across the city and on buses and subway cars. The goal was to get the story to the public and move bargaining from the back rooms of political dealing—where the local feared they would lose—into the public sphere.

The local garnered widespread support, including editorials in both the *Boston Globe* and the *Boston Herald* urging the mayor to settle with the union. Rather than attacking the mayor, the union appealed to Flynn, who had won the mayor's office on a platform focusing on "the everyday people." The "We're Worth It" Campaign made it difficult to ignore the nurses, the clerks, and the everyday people who provided important services to the city.

After tough bargaining the threat of a citywide strike loomed in April. After an entire weekend of round-the-clock bargaining, local members filled Fanieul Hall waiting for word from the bargaining committee. Picket captains had been chosen and the workers were prepared to strike. In the end, however, the mayor admitted that SEIU members were worth it. Members of Local 285 agreed to a contract in April, with the exception of nurses at Boston City Hospital who negotiated until September. The settlement included retroactive pay, wage increases, and an upgrade of annual step increases, as well an innovative contract language. It also reminded the residents of Boston of the importance of the services provided by city workers.

CHAPTER 16

University Workers Adopt New Tactics

THE 1970S AND 1980S SAW A DRAMATIC INCREASE in the number of women who entered the work force. Apart from the rising expectations and altered self-perceptions brought about by the women's movement, the most important reason why women entered the work force was economic necessity. This was as much the case for married women as it was for the growing number of female heads of household. In recent decades, declining real wages, together with the increasingly precarious position of male manufacturing workers, have made single-income families the exception rather than the norm. Women's earnings are essential to maintain family living standards. Growing numbers of women view themselves as permanent wage earners with a long-term stake in what happens at the workplace.

These developments created important opportunities for organizing. At a time when union membership was falling dramatically, organizing women became crucial to the survival of the labor movement. Yet stereotypes persisted about women being impossible to organize. Clerical workers in particular were viewed as unorganizable because they were not primary breadwinners in their families, because they were close to management, and because they held elitist "white-collar" values hostile to unions. Some important exceptions could be found in Massachusetts among the unionized women office workers employed by the gas, electric, and telephone utilities, but the old stereotypes about office workers remained.

A clerical worker at Boston University.

By the 1970s, however, women office workers began questioning their privileged status. In 1971, a survey published in the *Harvard Business Review* concluded that office workers "no longer bought the myth that management would take good care of them" and held "a much more negative impression of their employers than office workers surveyed in the past." During the 1970s, these workers protested publicly against pay discrimination, disrespect, and sexual harassment. In 1972, Nine to Five, a new organization formed in Boston, attracted growing support from unorganized women office workers. By the end of the decade, unions began to see issues in new ways and to develop new approaches to women clerical workers.

In the postwar era, union organizing had depended primarily on the "plant gate" model. Once contacted by workers interested in joining a union, organizers responded by leafleting at the plant gate and passing out union authorization cards. This model worked reasonably well as long as employers mounted little opposition to unions. But this changed in the 1970s, when management aggressively employed both legal and illegal tactics, including captive-audience meetings with employees, supervisor one-on-one meetings, threats, surveillance, and outright firings.

Library staff at Boston University.

Yet, despite this intense employer opposition, some unions organized new members, including District 65 at Boston University. After an initial drive ended in a 1971 election loss, organizing resumed three years later when university administrators introduced a new pay system that abolished cost-of-living increases and based wage hikes entirely on merit. In response, workers formed the Staff Committee against the Merit Plan, which subsequently affiliated with District 65. The next several years saw slow but steady advances as a result of the union's activist approach to organizing and the use of grassroots strategies that mobilized rank and filers. Instead of simply coming in to sign new members, the union created committees of workers that represented the make-up of the work force at Boston University. Anticipating the kind of opposition workers would face in the months before union elections, the committees worked one-on-one with members, building commitment and inoculating workers against employer actions. These tactics culminated in a 1978 election victory for District 65 at Boston University. Because of continued resistance from university officials, it took two strikes the following year before the union was able to secure its first contract.

Although initially elated with their success, union leaders recognized that their work had only begun. Apart from its poor economic package, the contract made no provision for union security. Workers had the option of joining or not joining the union. Coupled with high turnover rates among university clericals, this raised serious concerns about the union's viability. At one point, no more than 300 workers in the 850-person bargaining unit were dues-paying members. To meet the crisis, union activists redoubled the one-on-one techniques used during the organizational drive. These involved

WILD Women

Although a number of clerical and hospital worker organizing campaigns proved successful in Massachusetts, the campaigns highlighted the lack of women in leadership positions in the labor movement. Concerned about the small number of women labor leaders, a group of women labor activists and educators, including members of the Boston Coalition of Labor Union Women (CLUW), the Massachusetts AFL-CIO, and staff at the University of Massachusetts's labor programs, met to plan a strategy for an ongoing program of leadership development. In June 1987 the Women's Institute for Leadership Development (WILD) was formed and offered its first summer school program. WILD brought more than one hundred Massachusetts union women to Clark University in Worcester for a weekend of workshops and meetings.

Building on the tradition of union women's summer schools from the 1930s, WILD offered training in basic union skills such as grievance handling and organizing, as well as education directed specifically at women including sexual harassment and women's leadership. It also provided an opportunity for women to share stories, build friendships, and develop contacts.

Since the first summer more than seven hundred women from more than seventy union locals and a number of organizing drives have attended summer schools held annually on college campuses throughout the state. Between summer

schools WILD offers other opportunities for women to develop their leadership skills and abilities. Teacher-training workshops equip women to teach at WILD and in their own locals. Monthly breakfast meetings for labor activists provide a forum for these women to discuss issues and strategies and to find encouragement and support.

Now in its tenth year, WILD has made a difference in the development of women union leaders in Massachusetts. Many participants become instructors in the WILD program, work on summer school planning committees, and become members of the WILD board. Many of the women return home more informed and confident and become active in their locals. And, fulfilling the basic mission of WILD, many others have begun to take leadership roles in their locals and to assume important positions in the state and national labor movement.

maintaining regular contact with each worker, listening carefully to their observations on both union and workplace matters, helping to resolve any grievances they might have, and encouraging them to take an active part in union affairs. As they did, membership gradually rose, eventually stabilizing around the 500-member mark.

For union leaders, continued reliance on this grassroots, one-on-one model was not simply a means of ensuring organizational survival. It was also a reflection of the kind of union they hoped to create. As one handout put it: "We don't want to seem like all we care about is getting new members."

"There was real committed vision toward respect for each other," organizer Barbara Rahke remarked. This conviction was rooted in the leaders' own experience. Having themselves been subjected to various workplace indignities, they resolved "not to treat each other the way the boss treated us."

Besides creating an atmosphere of mutual respect, union leaders sought to increase members' awareness of their collective strength, to give them a sense of empowerment. The recollections of workers who became actively involved in union activities indicate that they succeeded. For some, it happened during protest rallies, "looking back behind you and seeing

One of many demonstrations during the organizing drive at Boston University.

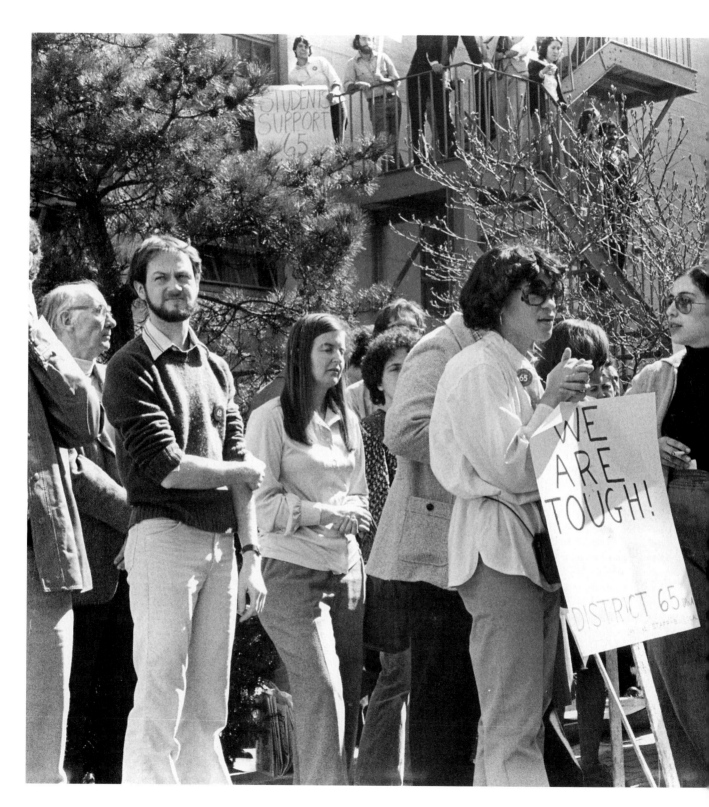

District 65 members demonstrating over stalled negotiations.

a long line of people together and hearing them shout and hearing [their voices] echo between the buildings." For others, it occurred at group discussions. "The meetings around negotiations had a big impact on me," Carol Gabin recalled. "There was a real sense of power and strength as workers. People really feeling like this was their forum to speak and really fight for what they wanted."

Many union activists had been strongly influenced by the women's movement, and their concerns were embodied in the organization's statement of principles, which declared: "Our union believes in and fights for full equality for women. We understand that full equality for women on the job is possible only when the roots and manifestations of sexism and racism in our whole society have been eliminated." To give meaning to these sentiments, union stewards aggressively pursued grievances involving sexual harassment and workplace customs that reinforced unflattering gender stereotypes. In so doing, they bolstered the assertiveness of women workers. As the workers came to realize that the union would be there for them, they began to take matters into their own hands. Recalling a case in which a secretary refused to make coffee for her department, union officer Beth Morrison remembered the inspiration she drew from watching this woman "stand up for herself and say I'm not going to do this, this isn't part of my job."

Another major concern of union officers was leadership development. To be effective, the one-on-one model requires a broad cadre of union activists who are constantly working to keep the membership in a state of mobilization. Again, the union's gender composition posed special challenges. As area coordinator Joan Bailey observed, many women "internalize a certain amount of helplessness" and frequently have to combat "lingering doubts" about themselves even after they have demonstrated a capacity for leadership. To help potential leaders overcome their reservations, the organization devised a mentoring program in which union veterans served as role models for promising newcomers. Women who went on to become union officers warmly appreciated this one-on-one attention. They also benefited from the organization's culture of openness and respect. Simply attending union meetings was a positive experience for many. "That's how I learned to think as a leader," Beth Morrison remarked, "by listening to other leaders thinking out loud, throwing ideas around, taking certain positions and then changing."

While they were trying to cultivate new leaders, union officers did not forget the general membership. A special committee, formed shortly after the organization's founding, sponsored a broad range of activities designed to reinforce rank and file commitment to union aims and principles. These activities included films, lectures, and slide shows on labor history and current events. Housing forums and a rape crisis training program helped members deal with problems outside the workplace. A newsletter, *Coffee Break*, served as a forum to explore such issues as day care, maternity leave, comparable worth, sexual harassment, and the traditional undervaluation of women's work. At the same time, the local organized softball teams and staged theatrical events. These initiatives led to the development of a vibrant union culture characterized by extensive rank and file involvement. It all paid off at contract time. With a highly mobilized membership behind them, union leaders achieved impressive gains at the bargaining table during the 1980s. On the economic front, they improved worker earnings by negotiating agreements that provided substantial across-the-board pay increases, raised minimum wages, and eliminated the lowest-paying job classifications.

As trade unionists in Massachusetts and across the country have discovered, this activist, grassroots model of organizing can be quite successful. And it need not be restricted to organizing women alone, but works well regardless of the make-up of the work force. As we have seen in the campaign at Boston University, this approach requires a great deal of effort and a fundamental change in union culture. But it allows rank and file workers to take ownership of their unions and become the labor movement's most effective representatives in reaching out to unorganized workers, the media, and the community.

PART VIII

New Challenges, New Strategies, 1981-1995

By the 1980s it was clear that a war was on against workers and unions across the country. Multinational corporations began leaving the United States in droves seeking lower wages and looser regulation in Central America, the Caribbean, and Southeast Asia. In a binge of corporate buying and selling in the 1980s, productive, economically viable companies were literally taken apart—raided for their most profitable operations, with the remains auctioned off to the highest bidder.

Companies with long historical roots in the United States simply left, and many products that had originated in this country, such as televisions, compact disks, and printed circuits, were no longer manufactured here. Between 1980 and 1990 alone, almost half a million manufacturing jobs were lost. The passage of the North American Free Trade Agreement (NAFTA) in 1994, against labor's strenuous objections, only exacerbated this trend.

With the election of Ronald Reagan in 1980, political power began to shift away from the Democratic party's New Deal coalition, in which workers and unions were a key element. In 1981, Reagan's firing of striking federal air traffic controllers and the breaking of their union, Professional Air Traffic Controllers Organization (PATCO), set the tone for how his administration would treat workers and unions. Workers' safety and health were compromised; the National Labor Relations Board (NLRB) was politicized, denying important protections to

unions; and many government regulations in support of workers and unions were weakened. The legitimacy of organizing labor in American society was under attack.

Encouraged by Reagan's assault and aided by changes in labor laws and regulations, employers reasserted their power in the workplace, employing a variety of legal and illegal means to block unionization if they could and break unions where they existed. A whole industry developed to help employers keep their workplaces "union free." The decade saw an exponential increase in the number of unfair labor practices filed by unions for illegal activity by employers, and by 1990 workers were illegally fired in one of every three organizing drives.

The Republican takeover of Congress in 1994, under the leadership of House Speaker Newt Gingrich, opened the way to complete the break with the New Deal. The Republican "Contract with America" sees unions only as obstacles to productivity and profit. Republicans have made a frontal attack on workers' safety and the prevailing wage and have proposed amending the National Labor Relations Act to allow "company unions," which have been outlawed since the 1930s. Legislation has even been introduced to roll back the eight-hour day and forty-hour week that three generations of workers struggled to attain. The Republican model for "reinventing government" advocates dismantling many New Deal and Great Society programs. By privatizing some programs and eliminating others, it would lead to a devastating loss of services and jobs in the public sector.

Union response to the nation's rapid deindustrialization, and to the attack on workers from both employers and government, was initially mixed. A generation of business unionism—filing grievances and negotiating contracts in a relatively secure environment—left labor organizations unprepared for the onslaught of corporate flight, employer intransigence, and government obstructionism. It became clear that the "bread and butter," "pure and simple" unionism inherited through the AFL lineage would not be enough to win in this hostile environment.

Yet important seeds of resurgence began to emerge across the nation as unions and workers adopted aggressive and innovative tactics in order to survive. In the struggles against J. P. Stevens, Eastern Airlines, the *New York Daily News*, the Pittston Coal group, and in campaigns such as Justice for Janitors, the labor movement was learning and applying a variety of new approaches. What links these campaigns together is that they all share a broader vision of trade unionism.

Many were community-based campaigns whose goals went far beyond bread-and-butter issues. Rooted in workers' communities, most used grass-roots organizing strategies and mobilized rank and file members as active participants. Slowly, more traditional business unionism was being replaced by an organizing model that saw each and every activity of the union as an opportunity to mobilize members and allies. These campaigns were not restricted to manufacturing or to white male workers. Indeed, some of the most exciting campaigns involved women and people of color in both the public and private sectors.

The 1980s saw an enormous amount of innovative union activity in Massachusetts and the rebirth of a vibrant labor movement. Local 277 of the United Electrical Workers challenged Gulf and Western's decision to close the profitable Morse Twist Drill Company in New Bedford, mounting a community-based campaign that ultimately led to the plant's being reopened. Boston school-bus drivers organized with the Steelworkers. Subways were covered with "We're Worth It" posters in a campaign that SEIU and AFSCME fought and won against the city of Boston. The yellow bumper stickers of Local 26 of the Hotel and Restaurant Workers Union's "Justicia" campaign were everywhere. In a stunning victory, clerical workers organized at Boston University, and even Harvard University went union.

What is more important, these were not just individual battles waged by individual unions. The 1980s witnessed an enormous growth of solidarity and mutual support by Massachusetts unions and workers. When major strikes and struggles erupted throughout the 1980s, even in faraway places such as the coalfields of Appalachia, Massachusetts workers and their unions responded. This is exactly what happened in both the campaign against Bay State Smelting and in the campaign to defeat the challenge to the prevailing wage in Massachusetts.

The increased activism of the Massachusetts AFL-CIO was central to revitalizing a unified labor movement in Massachusetts. Beginning with the election of Arthur Osborn as president in 1979, the state federation began rebuilding its ties with its affiliated unions and increasing its involvement in the political process. There is no better example than the 1988 campaign to defeat Question 2, a measure that would have rolled back the state's prevailing-wage law. Pulling together a broad-based coalition of unionists from across the Commonwealth, the state federation played a central role in organizing an impressive campaign that defeated a very powerful and well-funded special interest fueled by a nation-wide wave of tax-cutting measures.

Meanwhile, public employees and their unions faced a direct assault by conservative tax-cutting groups and by the trend toward privatization of government services. The passage in 1980 of Proposition 2½ on a referendum ballot drastically limited local property taxes and led to devastating layoffs of teachers, police officers, firefighters, and other public servants. Ten years later the public employee unions, led by the Massachusetts AFL-CIO, responded much more effectively to another tax-cutting referendum. The Tax Equity Alliance of Massachusetts (TEAM), supported by unions and a variety of public interest groups, relied on intensive grassroots organizing to educate the public and to create an alternative to destructive tax cutting. The progressive coalition persuaded the voters that the 1990 tax reduction went too far and cut too deep. Workers in the building trades, who had been supported in their 1988 campaign to save the prevailing wage, returned the favor by supporting the public sector workers.

The involvement of the State Federation of Labor grew dramatically with the election of Robert Haynes as secretary-treasurer in 1987 and of Joseph Faherty as president in 1991. The growing political power of the state federation under Faherty and Haynes was put to a severe test in the 1994 reelection of Massachusetts Senator Edward Kennedy. A staunch supporter of working people and their issues for a whole generation of Bay Staters, Kennedy faced

a fierce election battle. Riding the Republican wave of change that swept many Democratic incumbents from office, challenger Mitt Romney's campaign was heavily financed by national Republican interests. Union activists were mobilized across the Commonwealth, registering voters, distributing materials, and getting out the vote. In what was an extremely tight race to the very end, Kennedy won, with the support of the labor movement being key to the victory.

The national labor movement was also making important internal changes. Richard Trumka was elected on a rank-and-file slate as president of the United Mine Workers of America in 1981 and Ron Carey became president of the Teamsters Union in 1991, reclaiming these unions from a history of corruption and violence. The election of John Sweeney from the Service Employees International Union (SEIU) as the new president of the AFL-CIO in October 1995, along with Richard Trumka (UMWA) as secretary-treasurer and Linda Chavez-Thompson (AFSCME) as vice president, provides new hope for the labor movement. With an aggressive program committed to diversity, organizing, and building community coalitions, the labor movement is returning to the inclusiveness and social unionism of the Knights of Labor, the IWW, and the early CIO.

The challenges that face workers and unions across the nation and in the Commonwealth of Massachusetts will undoubtedly continue. Yet the labor movement has begun to plant the seeds of renewal in Massachusetts and across the country. And the struggle will continue for workers to make their lives and their communities more than simply a Commonwealth of Toil.

Hazardous material training conducted by MassCOSH.

CHAPTER 17

Protecting Health and Safety

FROM ITS EARLIEST DAYS, THE MASSACHUSETTS labor movement sought to protect workers from the dangers of industrial labor. Its leaders demanded state factory inspections, secured a law extending limited liability to employers for injured workers, and modified a workers' compensation law originally proposed by business. But still the toll mounted. One 1915 study estimated that at least twenty-five thousand workers died that year from work-related "accidents." Massachusetts workers suffered their share of tragedy in mill towns such as Lowell and Lawrence, as well as in the deadly railroad and construction industries.

Widespread unionization between 1935 and 1965 reduced workplace deaths significantly, as did improved state inspections. Between 1963 and 1971 about fourteen thousand workers lost their lives each year in the United States—still an appalling number when compared with European workplaces. The enactment of the federal Occupational Safety and Health Act in 1970 and the creation of an agency to enforce the law promised significant improvements. But now the public began to learn that occupational hazards took an even greater toll than most people realized. In 1972, a presidential report discovered that "at least 390,000 new cases of disabling occupational disease" developed each year and that an estimated 100,000 workers died of those diseases annually. In Massachusetts, unions relied on the Occupational Safety and Health Administration (OSHA) and the state Department of Labor and Industries to expand protection. They also received valuable assistance from MassCOSH,

a coalition of unions and health, scientific, and legal professionals.

Unionized workers at Boston Edison were deeply concerned about their health and safety. The 1,800 members of Local 369, Utility Workers of America, responsible for keeping electricity flowing to Boston Edison's 600,000 customers, found themselves frequently exposed to asbestos, radiation, high voltage fields, and a broad range of toxic substances. As union statistics attest, it is dangerous work. Between 1978 and 1986, eighty-eight members died of work-related injuries. Many retirees suffer from disabilities incurred during their years on the job.

Long concerned about health and safety matters, Local 369 president Donald Wightman joined with Joseph Faherty, whose Local 387 represented the clerical workers and meter readers, to make health and safety paramount in the 1986 contract talks with Boston Edison. Faherty, who became president of the Massachusetts AFL-CIO in 1991, had already joined with Nine to Five in seeking legislation to protect clerical workers from radiation and other hazards from video-display terminals. Faherty and Wightman asked the company to form a joint labor-management safety and health committee to monitor working conditions, hire additional staff to operate a comprehensive preventive maintenance program, maintain the wage rates of injured employees who had been reassigned to lower-paying positions, and provide improved benefit protection to disabled retirees and to the spouses and children of workers killed on the job.

Union leaders believed their demands were more

Joseph Faherty, president of the Massachusetts AFL-CIO and former president of Local 387 Utility Workers.

The union was well prepared for a work stoppage. For the previous several years, members had been making weekly contributions to a "Workers Investing in Negotiations" (WIIN) program. When the strike began on May 16, there was sufficient money in the fund to provide each member with $150 a week for nearly two months. Strikers were also eligible for unemployment benefits. The union waged the battle on a number of fronts. They blocked company efforts to prevent picketing at contractors' gates, forcing Boston Edison to stop construction work during the walkout. Meanwhile, union publicity initiatives, which highlighted the health and safety concerns of utility workers, gave Locals 387 and 369 a decided edge in the contest for public opinion. According to one striker: "It seemed that for the first time the general public was behind us, that for the first time they understood our plight and offered their support by either stopping and talking to us or by driving by our picket lines and beeping and waving to us."

Company executives began to realize that imposing concessions required more than a seemingly favorable climate of opinion. With setbacks mounting on all fronts, they reconsidered their position and returned to the bargaining table. In the final settlement, union leaders obtained most of their health and safety demands, as well as substantial wage increases. This would have been a good contract at any time, but during an era of givebacks, when most labor organizations were on the defensive, it was a major achievement. As Joseph Faherty remarked after his local ratified the new contract: "We are returning to work with our safety and our dignity protected, and we are returning without making any concessions."

Struggles over occupational health and safety continued into the 1990s as new groups of workers

than reasonable. During the previous year, Boston Edison had amassed record earnings of $94 million, and its return on shareholder equity was higher than that of most firms in the utility industry. Hoping to capitalize on the anti-union sentiment of the Reagan era, the company not only rejected the union's proposals but asked for concessions. Union negotiators recognized that their management counterparts had no real interest in reaching an equitable settlement, and their frustration and anger grew. Local 369's well-informed and highly mobilized membership felt much the same way and voted to strike.

became conscious of hazards. A Somerville firm with a long history of worker abuse and environmental pollution, Bay State Smelting Company, had attracted the attention of state and federal agencies on a number of occasions. In each instance, the company promised to clean up its operations and take appropriate steps to provide for the health and safety of its workers. But promising was all it did. Pollution of the surrounding community continued, as did the poisoning of its largely immigrant work force of Central Americans.

In December 1990, Gabriel García, a Bay State Smelting employee, sensing that something was terribly wrong at the plant, contacted OSHA. He had been experiencing problems with his eyes and kidneys, and he wanted OSHA "to visit the factory and discover the truth about the conditions we were working under." Though he did not provide his name—"because in the past a worker had called OSHA, and was fired when the bosses found out"— the agency responded, conducting investigations in January and May of 1991. The May 1991 inspection gave the company a clean bill of health. It did so largely because Bay State workers were unwilling or unable to inform OSHA officials of the problems in the plant. "If there had been a way for us to be more

Gabriel García *(seated on left)* and fellow workers from Bay State Smelting.

Massachusetts

This song by Greenfield, Massachusetts–based folksinger John O'Connor
captures the history of a factory family and the pain of the factory shutdowns
that became commonplace in the 1970s and 1980s.

I was born in Massachusetts,
In a company town in '43.
My father's shift was in the foundry,
My mother raised six kids and me.

Oh the blood of immigrants and workers,
Who came here ninety years ago.
Flows through these veins in Massachusetts,
In the town my grandfather used to know.

Well I never saved for an education,
It was pocket money that I made.
But at seventeen it seemed quite natural,
To take my place in my father's trade.

I started to raise myself a family,
With a blue-eyed girl that married me.
My mother helped us with the baby,
My father died at sixty-three.

When contract time came one November,
We couldn't believe what we had heard.
To take away all that we worked for,
To cut wages by full one-third.

Oh the strike was on before we knew it,
The company hit us from every side.
I never thought they could hurt us that bad,
Or realize how the papers lied.

Oh the weeks and months went by so slowly,
We swore to see the strike clear through.
But the company budged not one iota,
As if to break each one in two.

In the seventh month we got the bad news,
Sam Hawkins walked up soberly.
He told us how the strike was over,
They were moving the mill down to Tennessee.

Oh the blood of immigrants and workers,
Who came here ninety years ago.
Flows through these veins in Massachusetts,
In the town my grandfather used to know.

Give me your poor and huddled masses,
And your tired yearning to breathe free.
Then move them to the mills of Massachusetts,
And take away their jobs and their dignity.

Ann Philbin and Luz Rodriguez of IRATE and Victoria Martinez of MassCOSH.

involved, in a way that we were not risking our jobs," García said, "we could have all told this inspector what was really going on." But they couldn't because they were afraid of being fired. In fact, García's outspokenness about company safety practices resulted in a "layoff" that was doubtless intended to reinforce worker fears. "The reason people are afraid to speak out," he later remarked, "is that they see what happens to people like me." Worse, he added: "As long as this continues you will always have workplaces like Bay State Smelting Company. Workers will continue to lose their health, lose their jobs, and lose their lives."

As Nancy Lessin of MassCOSH observed: "Death in the workplace is too often the 'perfect crime.' No one is held accountable; no penalty is paid by the perpetrator." This instance, however, would be different. During the same month that García wrote OSHA, a neighborhood health center physician called MassCOSH about a Spanish-speaking Bay State employee who was lead-poisoned. MassCOSH

had recently instituted a Latino Workers Health and Safety Project that often worked together with the Boston-based Immigrant Rights Advocacy, Training, and Education Project (IRATE), now called the Immigrant Workers Resource Center (IWRC).

Over the next several months, representatives from MassCOSH and IRATE established a close relationship with Bay State employees, providing them with information and training on the handling of toxic substances. They arranged for further inspections by state and federal authorities. The results of these inquiries—which began in June, just a month after the second OSHA visit—were considerably different from the earlier investigations. This time, workers actively assisted the inspectors, telling them where to look and what they were likely to discover. Among other violations, investigators found that Bay State employees were routinely exposed to dangerously high levels of lead, carbon monoxide, and other toxic substances; they were not provided proper protective gear; and they had no hot water to wash the various toxins from their skin. They were also required to perform work that contaminated the surrounding neighborhood during the evening hours, when pollution was less detectable, and they were forced to dump hazardous wastes in ways that endangered both them and the environment.

Needless to say, working conditions at Bay State could hardly have deteriorated so greatly between May and June. Empowered by the support they received from MassCOSH and IRATE, the workers decided that it was time to follow Gabriel García's example. And once they did, there was no longer any conceivable way Bay State executives could conceal what they were doing. "The unforgettable lesson of this," Nancy Lessin said, "is that workers themselves are the true experts about what goes on in their workplaces. They know their workplace, and their work, like no one else."

It was certainly a lesson for Bay State owners, who afterward paid dearly for their transgressions. That December, OSHA hit the company with fines totaling $214,500. By OSHA standards, this was an unusually large amount for a small business to be penalized. In March 1994, as the result of an ongoing state investigation by the Environmental Strike Force, Judge Katherine Liacos Izzo levied an additional $500,000 fine. She also sentenced Bay State's president and plant manager to 750 hours of labor similar to that performed by company employees.

Worker advocacy groups used the case to demonstrate the need for an effective "whistleblower" bill to protect wage earners who exposed unsafe workplace conditions. The subsequent passage of such a measure by the Massachusetts House and Senate provided an altogether fitting conclusion to the Bay State story. As MassCOSH's Lessin said of the Izzo decision, the people who deserve "credit for this conviction are the courageous workers who lost their jobs bringing a health and safety issue to the attention of public officials."

Nancy Lessin testified before a July 1993 hearing of the House Subcommittee on Labor Standards, Occupational Health and Safety. "Today in Massachusetts, 200 more workers will be injured severely enough to lose five or more days from work. This week, we can predict two workers will leave for their jobs and never return home to their families. And this month, more than 100 Massachusetts workers will be diagnosed with work-related cancer."

Despite more than a century of reform, American workplaces remain hazardous. While the creation of OSHA has significantly lowered fatalities, many hazardous workplaces remain. The startling array of toxic industrial substances that have been developed in the past half-century pose dangers to contemporary workers that were largely unknown to their predecessors. But what has not changed is employer reluctance to spend the money needed to ensure safe working conditions. Indeed, many corporate spokespersons increasingly argue that occupational safety laws are incompatible with the nation's survival as a major industrial power. Unfortunately, much work remains to be done. Nancy Lessin was simply stating a grim truth when she told congressional investigators: "Productivity and competitiveness are the watchwords of the day. Profits and short-term gain are paramount. Workers are expendable."

CHAPTER 18

Massachusetts Building Trades Fight Back

T HE DECADE OF THE 1980S WAS A BLEAK TIME for American workers. At the bargaining table, employers used their increased leverage to exact a variety of givebacks from embattled union negotiators. And in the political arena, anti-union groups conducted a broad-ranging attack on protective labor legislation at both the state and federal levels.

In Massachusetts, a major target of such groups was the Commonwealth's prevailing-wage law. Enacted in 1914, the statute required that workers on state-financed building projects be paid the same wage rates as local unionists. In 1931, Congress passed a similar measure, the Davis-Bacon Act, which covered all federal construction. The main purpose of these laws was to stabilize labor costs in a ruthlessly competitive industry whose boom-and-bust nature offered little security to either workers or

Labor Day in Marlborough, 1988.

contractors and to ensure quality construction. By setting a fair wage rate, contracts for public construction could be awarded based on the competence of the construction company, its quality and productivity, rather than the lowest price.

Building tradespeople welcomed the legislation. So did union contractors, who were already paying the mandated rates and who bitterly resented being underbid by their non-union counterparts. Non-union contractors strongly opposed the laws, though lack of organization long prevented their doing much about them. Davis-Bacon and related state measures encountered no serious opposition for decades after their passage. All this started to change during the 1970s, when the Associated Builders and Contractors (ABC), with assistance from the powerful Business Roundtable, made repeal of prevailing-wage legislation the centerpiece of a broader open-shop drive. The campaign, which began at mid-decade, compiled a mixed record at the federal level. In Congress, efforts to overturn Davis-Bacon proved unsuccessful; but with the election of Ronald Reagan, ABC lobbyists received a sympathetic hearing in the executive branch. In 1982 Secretary of Labor Raymond Donovan issued regulations that weakened the enforcement of the federal statute.

Meanwhile, a simultaneous state-based drive had already achieved its first success a year earlier when Utah repealed its prevailing-wage law. Afterward, ABC attention centered on Massachusetts. It did so for several reasons. One was the size and political savvy of the organization's Massachusetts/Rhode Island chapter, whose president, Stephen Tocco, had a well-deserved reputation for being able to link contractor interests to those of the general public. Another was the Commonwealth's strong union heritage. A victory there, ABC officials reasoned, would "set a precedent with national implications."

As they had done at the federal level, ABC leaders focused initially on the legislature, with much the same results. Both houses were controlled by Democratic politicians, most of whom wanted no part of a bill that threatened to destroy the state's building trades unions. Recognizing that they needed a new approach, ABC officials decided to follow the example set by one of their leading allies, Citizens for Limited Taxation (CLT), whose successful 1980 referendum effort had capped local property taxes in Massachusetts. In so doing, they also adopted the CLT's tax-cutting theme. Abolishing the state's prevailing-wage law, they argued, would eliminate a major drain on state and local revenue. It was a popular message that many media sources uncritically echoed. And by December 1987, the ABC campaign organization, which after a series of name changes was now calling itself the Fair Wage Committee, had collected enough signatures to place the repeal question on the following year's ballot.

Construction unionists had not been idle while all this was happening. Their initial response was to form a statewide hotline that enabled them to dispatch members to sites where ABC operatives were collecting signatures for the ballot measure. Once there, union representatives were frequently able to counter ABC claims about tax savings by demonstrating that the organization was only interested in slashing worker wages. Union leaders also

circulated two initiative petitions of their own, which were designed to shift the debate from high wages to excess profits and exorbitant interest rates. Neither tactic worked. The hotline slowed down the ABC referendum effort but did not prevent its ultimate success. And the unions failed to gather sufficient signatures to put their own questions on the ballot.

With these developments, a sense of gloom settled over union halls across Massachusetts. "We were pretty depressed," Joe Dart, president of the Pioneer Valley Building Trades Council, later said of this period. "We felt we'd done a good job stopping them in the western part of the state, but we still lost the overall battle and were moving into an even more ominous situation." Early public opinion surveys showed widespread support for the ABC initiative. According to one union poll, voters favored repeal by a decisive 49 to 30 percent margin. Yet, however bleak their prospects, union officials knew that this was no time to feel sorry for themselves. They still had a job to do. As IBEW business agent Rich Gambino recalled, "Our failure scared us and, I think, ultimately motivated us."

One source of that motivation was the embarrassment caused by the ABC victory. "After all," Gambino added, "they had no organization, and we supposedly did." It was a telling observation, for union leaders quickly recognized that they first had to put their own house in order. The hotline and referenda efforts had in large part been top-down initiatives that did little to educate, much less mobilize, rank and filers. And without their active and enthusiastic support in the months ahead, chances of reversing voter opinion on the prevailing-wage question were slim indeed.

To turn things around, the first step unions took was to levy a fifty-dollar assessment on all members.

Harvard clerical and technical workers supporting the fight against Question 2.

Apart from providing needed funds, the levy gave rank and filers a tangible stake in the upcoming campaign. "We obviously needed the money," one union official remarked, "but it could have been raised in a number of ways. The assessment created a psychological investment." At the same time, union leaders initiated a voter registration drive. Voting had been on the decline nationally for some years, and Bay State construction workers followed the trend. "What we found was amazing," said Russ Sheehan of the IBEW. "When our coordinator for the town of Whitman contacted the twenty IBEW members who lived there, for example, he discovered that only five were registered." This was truly an alarming problem. Unionists and their immediate families made up nearly one-third of the state's population, and it was absolutely essential that substantial numbers of them show up at the polls in November. The registration drive not only helped ensure that this would happen, it also prepared volunteers for future tasks. As Rick Brown of Gloucester put it: "Doing voter registration introduced me to a lot of people in my town that I ended up counting on later, and I started thinking real hard about what lay ahead."

In addition to mobilizing their members, union

Local 26 Changes the Lives of Hotel Workers

In the 1980s, four thousand hotel workers from Boston's finest and oldest hotels captured the hearts and minds of the city. Members of Hotel and Restaurant Employees Union Local 26, these maids, waiters, bellhops, desk clerks, dishwashers, laundry workers, chefs, and doormen in 1982, and then again in 1985 and 1988, took on hotels such as the Ritz-Carlton, Copley Plaza, and Parker House, and won. During those years, bright yellow banners, buttons, balloons, and bumper stickers, displaying nothing more than the word "Justice" in English, Spanish, and French, could be seen on telephone poles, newspaper stands, subway stops, and the lapels and automobiles of citizens across the city. Local unions from the building trades to the Service Employees each adopted a hotel, committing to walk the picket lines, staff the strike kitchens, and organize public support. Public officials and even the major TV stations and newspapers called on the hotels to settle with the union and avoid a strike. And in their ultimate triumph, by the end of the decade Local 26 had not only negotiated the first employer-paid housing trust fund in the United States but it had successfully lobbied the U.S. Congress to amend the Taft-Hartley Act to make such trust funds a permissible subject of bargaining.

Until 1980, little had been heard from these workers, inside or outside of the labor movement. Despite the fact that the majority of hotel workers were immigrant women and people of color,

Members of Local 26 on one of many picket lines.

working in "back of the house" jobs as housekeepers, kitchen aides, or laundry workers, the union had long been dominated by "front of the house" workers: the bartenders, doormen, and concierges, all primarily white men. But then, in 1980, the back of the house took over the union when a reform slate of officers, led by Dominic Bozzotto, gained control and began to take on the Boston hotels.

Before doing so the union had to break down the barriers within its own membership. Not only were there age-old occupational divisions, but there were ethnic and language divisions as well. Two-thirds of the membership were women and two-thirds of them were women of color. Many were very recent immigrants. More than eighty different languages were spoken among the four thousand Local 26 members.

The union started by having its literature and meetings translated into each of the four major languages—Creole, Spanish, Portuguese, and English—spoken by the membership. A 350- to 500-person contract action committee and a 50-person bargaining committee were chosen, representative of all the different interest groups in the unit. Coalitions were built with other unions, civil rights organizations, politicians, and community groups.

They faced stiff opposition from the Boston hotel owners, who time and again backed down only when they were faced with a citywide hotel strike during the busiest season. Starting with simple justice issues, such as ending "English only" requirements on the job and rules obligating hotel maids to clean bathroom floors on their hands and knees, the union was able to make significant wage and benefit gains with each contract, for the first time bringing their lowest-paid members into line with wage scales at major hotels in other cities. All their efforts culminated in the 1988 campaign that forced hotel owners, many of whom were the wealthiest realtors in the city, to begin making contributions to a housing trust fund for their employees.

officials needed to give the general populace a reason for rejecting the repeal initiative. Through the spring of 1988, little had been done in this regard. As a consequence, ABC's dissemination of "horror stories" that depicted the prevailing-wage law as "legalized larceny" went largely unchallenged. To counter the lies and distortions on which such claims rested, the construction unions retained a nationally known research firm to conduct an independent examination of the law's effect on the Bay State economy. The study, released in August, forecast a marginal tax savings from repeal and concluded that the "only clear result" of eliminating the statute "would be lower wages for Massachusetts residents." These findings were a severe blow to the ABC's credibility. They also enabled union leaders to redefine the prevailing-wage question. What had been a tax dispute now became a debate over contractor profits and the living standards of working people.

This redefinition of the prevailing-wage issue also helped construction unionists get support from the broader community. Because of their long-standing tradition of going it alone—a product of what carpenter-historian Mark Erlich has called an "insider" versus "outsider" mentality—the building trades had begun the campaign with few allies. Even their relationships with other unions were weak. Eight years earlier, for example, the struggle to defeat the CLT's tax-cutting initiative had received little assistance from construction unions. Municipal workers, many of whom lost jobs as a consequence of the measure's passage, still remembered the unions' inactivity.

During the campaign, supporters of Question 2 made a special effort to capitalize on these divisions in the labor movement, appealing directly to public workers. In a typical statement, Richard Boutiette of the Massachusetts Highway Association declared:

Susan Eisenberg is a Boston-based writer who graduated from IBEW Local 103's apprenticeship program in the first class to contain women.

PIONEERING

for the tradeswomen of '78
Susan Eisenberg

She had walked into their party uninvited
wedging a welcome mat in the doorway
for other women she hoped would
follow along soon.
          The loud ones argued
to throw her out immediately. Even her supporters
found her audacity annoying. But once they saw
     she mingled with everyone
     drank American beer
     kept conversations going during awkward silences

     and was backed up by law
the controversy
        calmed.

She surprised them.
She was reliable. She always gave her best.
She was invited back.
She became a regular —
     always on the fringe
     expected to help out
        just a little more.

When she stopped coming
they were confused. Why now? Hadn't she
challenged custom? stared down rumors? ingratiated herself
years ago? so that now her presence was only
mildly discomforting. She never explained.

After all those years hurling back cannonballs
womanizing the barricades firing
only if she saw the whites of their eyes
it was the lonesomeness
          of pioneering
that broke her resistance.

All those silences
     about what mattered
      most in her life
had worn her,

like the slow eating away of acid on metal:
the damage only visible over time.

Some of the 100,000 signs being prepared for distribution as part of the campaign against Question 2.

"Many of the municipal workers or teachers threatened with layoffs wouldn't be if the town wasn't forced to waste money on artificially inflated wages." As it turned out, most public workers found the construction unions' counterclaims much more compelling. "When our workers were appealed to as working people," Nancy Mills of the SEIU observed, "they understood that it was in their best interest" to support the building trades. They also knew that Citizens for Limited Taxation was a prominent ABC ally. "You just mentioned [CLT president] Barbara Anderson's name and their heads snapped," a Salem electrician recalled. "They recognized this as an

attack on all organized labor and [a no vote on Question 2] was a way of getting even."

As the campaign progressed, the construction unions' outreach activities proved increasingly successful. Major political figures such as Governor Michael Dukakis, Senators John Kerry and Edward Kennedy, and Boston Mayor Ray Flynn weighed in on behalf of the building trades. Numerous school committees and city councils passed resolutions denouncing Question 2, leaders of the state's senior community pledged their assistance, and, on college campuses, students did their part to spread the union message. Even most public housing advocates came on board, despite the fact that the prevailing-wage law added to construction costs. As Tom Cunha, president of the Charlestown Economic Development Corporation, asked: "How do you build affordable public housing if the people you're building it for can't afford to buy it?"

Construction unionists also obtained support from organizations representing women and people of color. This was a particularly significant breakthrough. The building trades had a reputation as a white male bastion whose membership had never shown any enthusiasm for affirmative action programs. Yet, as union officials demonstrated, the gender and ethnic composition of the construction work force had become increasingly diverse in recent years. These advances, coupled with the justice of their cause, enabled them to secure endorsements from a broad range of groups. National Organization for Women president Molly Yard found it "ironic that as the construction trades are opening up to women, the owners should try to repeal the long-standing prevailing-wage structure which provides a decent wage." The state's Black Legislative Caucus issued a statement warning of "the devastating impact the repeal of prevailing wage would have on working people across the Commonwealth." And Cesar Chavez left no doubt about where he stood in a letter to his Massachusetts supporters: "Question 2 was placed on the ballot by the usual suspects—anti-union contractors, certain developers, and insurance interests. Their motivation never changes—it's greed. To them the best worker is an unorganized, underpaid worker."

In addition to their coalition-building initiatives, union leaders also put together an effective grassroots field organization. The key figures here were the union tradespeople and volunteer activists who served as town and ward coordinators. Their

Robert Haynes

A key player in the revival of the Massachusetts AFL-CIO is Secretary-Treasurer Bob Haynes. A tireless activist, Haynes promotes worker education and training, renewed effort in labor's involvement in the political process, and bringing the labor movement in Massachusetts back into the public eye.

A Cambridge native, Haynes grew up influenced by the unions that "everybody's parents in my neighborhood were involved in." When he started working at age sixteen, it was not by accident that Haynes found a union job in a grocery store. He went on to a number of other part-time union jobs. As Haynes recalls, "The union's were good to me when I was a kid."

While in college he began working summers as an ironworker, also a union job. In 1970 he decided that he "liked busting rod a whole lot more than chemistry" and went to work full time in the industry. He enrolled in the Ironworkers' apprentice program in 1973 and by 1979 had become secretary-treasurer of his Ironworkers' local. He later obtained a B.S. from Boston State College and an M.B.A. from the University of Massachusetts Boston. Always active in the Massachusetts labor movement, he became secretary-treasurer of the state AFL-CIO in 1987.

As education director of the state Federation, Haynes convened a statewide education program in 1988 and invited a broad range of trade unionists and educators to help chart the direction of the Massachusetts AFL-CIO. Having gone through an apprentice program himself, Haynes appreciated the value of training and he knew how important it was for the labor movement to play a strong role in the educational process.

Robert Haynes, secretary-treasurer of the Massachusetts AFL-CIO and a key leader in the defeat of Question 2.

Central to this effort was a push from Haynes to have labor representatives appointed to the board of trustees of state universities and community colleges and the boards of directors of state agencies that oversaw training. Under the administration of Governor Michael Dukakis, who embraced these efforts on the part of the Massachusetts AFL-CIO, Haynes was appointed trustee of the University of Massachusetts and labor was represented at every state university and community college except one. Labor was also successful in placing representatives in state training agencies, including appointing Massachusetts AFL-CIO members to the Massachusetts Jobs Council. With this new voice, the labor movement in the Commonwealth was given valuable influence in making education and training available to its members.

In 1995 Haynes led the effort to revive labor education at the University of Massachusetts. A statewide labor extension program was established and four new staff located on the Amherst, Boston, Lowell, and Dartmouth campuses provide regional and statewide training for Massachusetts workers.

Haynes continues to be a powerful voice for workers in Massachusetts, feeling strongly that "we need to be able to communicate how unions are fundamental for workers, our communities, and our families." He sees increasing the public's awareness of labor's role in society as labor's greatest challenge.

efforts during the campaign's final months substantially elevated public understanding of the prevailing-wage issue. These town and ward committees distributed union literature to every household in the state on two separate occasions, operated a system of phone banks that made 175,000 calls to prospective supporters, and put up posters across the Commonwealth. No less remarkable was the enthusiasm exhibited by the people who made all this possible. According to field coordinator Janice Fine: "They mobilized themselves. We just tried to keep up with the demand. It was an organizer's dream, something you just can't structure. It's the point at which an organization turns into a movement, when people just go off on their own."

Election day finally arrived, and at 7:00 A.M., at least one campaign supporter was stationed outside every polling place in the state. Later, as the returns rolled in, 58 percent of Massachusetts voters pulled the "No" lever on Question 2. It was a stunning victory that few people outside the labor movement had foreseen. Indeed, as late as 10:00 P.M., Boston's ABC-TV affiliate, Channel 5, had announced a different outcome.

By election day, the Bay State building trades were no longer the inward-looking organizations that they had been six months earlier. "Democracy in our unions may be a pain . . . sometimes," Jack Getchell of the Bricklayers later observed, "but it's our strong point. During the campaign, unions that operated on a top-down basis didn't respond as well. People need to have a tradition of being involved in order to take initiative." Union leaders also learned that, as secretary-treasurer of the Massachusetts AFL-CIO Robert Haynes put it, organized labor "can't do it alone." Mark Erlich of the Carpenters expressed it best when he wrote "the labor movement will arrest its decline and reassert its potential when it once again—as it has done in its finest hours—identifies unions with the desires and aspirations of the entire working community and with the broader crusade for social and economic justice."

52 "Judging from some of the reports" Albert A. Carlton in *Journal of United Labor*, quoted in Hartford, *Working People of Holyoke*, p. 80.

52 "This is the workingman's hour" Quoted in Green and Donahue, *Boston's Workers*, p. 37.

Chapter 7. The American Federation of Labor

54 Frank Foster quotations are from *Labor Leader*, Jan. 15, 1887; June 2, 1888; July 16, 1887; Feb. 4, 1888.

55 "general unity of purpose" Frank Foster in ibid., Jan. 14, 1888.

57 "one of the cases where the efficacy" Frank Foster in ibid.

57 "It was a grand pageant" *Boston Globe*, Sept. 5, 1887.

57 "the humble bootblack" in *Springfield Republican*, Sept. 3, 1901, quoted in Hartford, *Working People of Holyoke*, p. 109.

58 "Each year marks the growth" Woods, *The City Wilderness*, pp. 282–85.

58 "great improvement in all the conditions" Ibid.

60 "not less than the customary" Prevailing wage law quoted in Heintz and Whitney, *History of the Massachusetts Federation of Labor*, p. 94.

60 "Through the system of spying" *Worcester Labor News*, May 10, 1915.

Chapter 8. Irish Immigrants Build Holyoke

61 "the dam is leaking badly" Frank H. Doane, "History of Holyoke, Massachusetts from 1830 to 1870," ms. at Holyoke Public Library, n.d., p. 15, quoted in Hartford, *Working People of Holyoke*, p. 7.

64 "There is no such thing as steady employment" *Boston Globe*, Feb 21, 1921, in quoted in Erlich, *With Our Hands*, p. 4.

64 "As I pass up and down" Walter Stevenson, quoted in ibid., p. xiv.

65 "We should also like to know" *Holyoke Transcript*, June 9, 1892, quoted in ibid., p. 95.

69 "arbitrary spirit of the men" *Holyoke Transcript*, April 21, 1888, quoted in ibid., p. 91.

70 "One is the much celebrated rise" David Montgomery, "The Irish and the American Labor Movement," in *America and Ireland, 1776–1976: The American Identity and the Irish Connection*, ed. David Noel Doyle and Owen Dudley Edwards (Westport, CT: Greenwood Press, 1980), p. 212, in ibid., p. 93.

Chapter 9. The Strike for Bread and Roses in Lawrence

75 "The mills are Lawrence" in Massachusetts Consumer League Papers, Radcliffe College, Schlesinger Library,
Cambridge, Massachusetts, Account of Meeting on the Lawrence Strike in the Consumers League Office, March 8, 1919, box 25, folder 416, quoted in Goldberg, *A Tale of Three Cities*, p. 85.

75 "The little jests that break the monotony" and "would mean hiring only" Quoted in U.S. Immigration Commission, *Immigrants in Industries*, p. 772.

76 "I am willing that they should all" William Rae in Massachusetts Legislature, Joint Committee on Labor, *Hearing to Investigate the Causes of Recent Reductions of Wages in the Cotton Mills of Massachusetts* (1898), pp. 811–12, typescript at Museum of American Textile History, North Andover-Lowell, Massachusetts.

76 "We are a new people" in 62nd Congress. 2nd session, *Senate Document No. 870*, "Report on the Strike of the Textile Workers in Lawrence, Massachusetts, in 1912," (Washington, D.C.: U.S. Government Printing Office, 1912), p. 39, quoted in Dubofsky, *We Shall Be All*, p. 246.

78 "I would have kept on" and "but what would we eat" In U.S. House Representatives, *The Strike at Lawrence*, pp. 145, 153. 5 "The machinery was speeded up" Ibid., p. 35.

78 "There is no foreigner here" Bill Haywood, quoted in Peter Carlson, *Roughneck: The Life and Times of Big Bill Haywood* (New York: W. W. Norton, 1983), p. 165.

80 "The women won the strike" Bill Haywood quoted in Cameron, *Radicals of the Worst Sort*, p. 126.

81 "One cold morning" William D. Haywood, *Bill Haywood's Book: The Autobiography of Big Bill Haywood* (New York: International Publishers, 1929), p. 249, quoted in ibid., p. 148.

81 "They're everywhere" in Cameron, "Bread and Roses Revisited," p. 44.

86 "The fact of eighteen diverse nationalities" in Lorin F. Deland, "The Lawrence Strike: A Study," *Atlantic Monthly* 109 (May 1912): 705.

Chapter 10. The Women's Trade Union League and the Telephone Operators

88 "You had no life of your own" Mary Quinn Wynne interview with Stephen H. Norwood, Springfield, Massachusetts, June 28, 1974, in Norwood, *Labor's Flaming Youth*, p. 99.

88 "We couldn't whisper" in Green and Donahue, *Boston's Workers*, p. 95.

89 "The chief operator and other officials" Mary Quinn Wynne interview with Norwood, *Labor's Flaming Youth*, p. 107.

91 "full authority for separate self-government" "Proposed Constitution of the Telephone Operators' Department," Julia O'Connor Papers, Radcliffe College, Schlesinger Library, Cambridge, Massachusetts, quoted in ibid., p. 150.

92 "You never got any information" Rose Finklestein Norwood interview with Stephen H. Norwood, Boston, Massachusetts, May 2, 1975, in ibid., p. 226.

92 "maintain self-control and give opportunity" Samuel Gompers, in *Springfield Republican*, April 19, 1919.

92 "It took the Yankee Division" and "The utterance of this operator" *Boston Post*, April 12, 1919, quoted in Norwood, *Labor's Flaming Youth*, p. 180.

92 The Police Strike of 1919 All quotes from Robert K. Murray, *Red Scare: A Study of National Hysteria, 1919–20* (New York: McGraw-Hill, 1964). "a police officer," p. 123; "a crime against," p. 130; "There is no right," p. 132.

94 "If the corner grocer" *Springfield Republican*, April 19, 1919.

94 Monsignor James Cassidy in *Fall River Globe*, quoted in Norwood, *Labor's Flaming Youth*, p. 188.

94 "few days on the battle line" Julia S. O'Connor, "History of the Organized Telephone Operators' Movement," *Union Telephone Operator* (Jan.-March and May-July 1921), part 5, p. 16, quoted in ibid., pp. 194–95.

PART V: From Raw Deal to New Deal, 1920–1939

96 "Negro labor in the main" NAACP letter to AFL, quoted in Foner, *Organized Labor and the Black Worker*, p. 170.

Chapter 11. Surviving Hard Times

99 "The union had no protection" Enrico Porente quoted in Roboff, *Boston's Labor Movement*, p. 27.

99 "Landlords cut rents" Beatrice Pacheco quoted in Georgianna and Aaronson, *The Strike of '28*, p. 9.

99 "Lowell, Lawrence, New Bedford" Thomas McMahon quoted in Adamic, *My America*, pp. 263–64.

100 "More progressive, constructive" William Green quoted in Curley, *I'd Do It Again*, p. 270.

101 Sacco and Vanzetti "Not only am I innocent" Bartolomeo Vanzetti quoted in Jackson, *The Black Flag*. "permeated by prejudice" Michael Dukakis, *Boston Globe*, July 20, 1977.

103 "cursed by the awful chaos" Quoted in Adamic, *My America*, p. 264.

103 "get a shoe model that they think will sell" Ibid., p. 273.

105 "that whatever words I use" Martha Gellhorn to Harry Hopkins, undated report, "Visit to Massachusetts," Nov. 15–25, 1934, Hopkins Mss., Box 59, Franklin D. Roosevelt Library, Hyde Park, N.Y., quoted in Trout, *Boston: The Great Depression and the New Deal*, p. 174.

105 "You just had to keep traveling" Quoted in Erlich, *With Our Hands*, p. 114.

105 "went from street to street" Quoted in Nash, *From Tank Town to High Tech*, p. 71.

105 "We had nothing before" Sophie quoted in Blewett, *Surviving Hard Times*, p. 153.

106 "People like us who were poor" Ibid., p. 154. 5 "In spite of the rough times" Ibid., p. 155.

106 "People were good" Yvonne Hoar quoted in ibid., p. 136.

Chapter 12: The Birth of the CIO and the Revival of the AFL

108 "Better the occasional faults" Franklin D. Roosevelt quoted in Bollen, *Great Labor Quotations*, p. 103.

112 A. Philip Randolph and Black Railroad Workers All quotes from Green and Hayden, "A. Philip Randolph and Boston's African American Railroad Worker," in *Trotter Institute Review* 6, no. 1 (1992): 20–22.

113 "three progressive Negro" Pesotta, *Bread upon the Waters*, p. 322.

113 "very discouraging" Mary Sweet quoted in Banks, *First-Person America*, pp. 133–34.

PART VI: Labor in the Modern Commonwealth, 1940–1955

120 "the first savage thrust" John L. Lewis, in Green, *The World of the Worker*, p. 199.

Chapter 13: Labor in the War Years

121 "If you had a union book" in Erlich, *With Our Hands*, p. 131.

121 "Whoever is right" Gabe LaDoux interview, Nov. 4, 1983, "Oral History Project: The Mill Workers of Lawrence," Museum of American Textile History, North Andover-Lowell, Massachusetts.

121 "used to bawl you out" Rose Diamentina quoted in Donna Huse et al., "Vizinhanca: Neighborhood," *Spinner: People and Culture in Southeastern Massachusetts* 1 (1981): 17.

122 "I've decided that my place" In J. A. Miller, *Men and Volts at War* (New York: McGraw Hill Book Company, 1948), pp. 237–38, quoted in Nash, *From Tank Town to High Tech*, p. 82.

125 "they couldn't make ends meet" Dorothy Ahearn interview, March 8, 1976, in Miller, *The Irony of Victory*, p. 57.

125 "Gee, I got good money" Yvonne Hoar quoted in Blewett, *Surviving Hard Times*, p. 139.

126 "I knew nothing about machinery" Alice Swanton interview, June 4, 1975, in Miller, *The Irony of Victory*, pp. 63–64.

126 "substandard wages paid to women" "Extracts from the UE's Brief to the War Labor Board (in connection with the Westinghouse Electric Corp. and General Electric Company), Sept. 19, 1945, Records of the U.S. Women's Bureau, National Archives, Record Group 86, box 1599, quoted in Milkman, *Gender at Work*, p. 60.

126 "They put the boys back" in Nash, *From Tank Town to High Tech*, p. 84.

126 "surprising numbers expressed their eagerness" Green, *The Role of Women as Production Workers in War Plants in the Connecticut Valley*, p. 62.

128 "as obsolete as the water clock" In Sumner D. Charm, "Textile Twilight, New England," p. 1, Mss. 129A, file 1A, box 16, Research Department 1952 folder, Textile Workers Union of America Records, State Historical Society of Wisconsin, Madison, Wisconsin.

128 "Very few other unions" Solomon Barkin, "Economic Problems," ms., Sept. 14, 1956, Bound Notebook 10, Solomon Barkin Papers, W.E.B. Du Bois Library, University of Massachusetts at Amherst, Amherst, Massachusetts.

128 "Where is our responsibility?" Solomon Barkin, in Minutes, Departmental Directors Meeting, Nov. 5, 1954, Mss. 129A, file 1A, box 5, Textile Workers Union of America Records.

Chapter 14: Boston's Packinghouse Workers

130 "longest union meeting on record" Quoted in Bollen and Miller, *The Colonial Strike*, p. 21.

130 "Local 11 was born of strikes" John Mitchell in videotaped interview, Sept. 17, 1984, in Labor Collection, Healey Library Archives, University of Massachusetts at Boston, quoted in Bollen and Green, "The Long Strike," pp. 236, 241.

130 "persecute militant union members" Jim Bollen, in "Lynn Unionist to Defy Red Quiz Today," *Boston Globe*, Oct. 4, 1954, quoted in ibid., p. 240.

131 "news blackout" Jim Bollen, in Roboff, *Boston's Labor Movement*, p. 61.

132 "been cut down by 40%" Ibid., p. 63.

133 "If it takes six months or six years" Ralph Helstein quoted in Bollen and Miller, *The Colonial Strike*, p. 11.

134 "only pressure from inside the plant" Quoted in ibid., p. 11.

135 "part of the community" Shelton Coats, in "Glory Days" video (produced by Cynthia McKeown), quoted in Bollen and Green, "The Long Strike," p. 247.

136 "made by Negroes in the labor movement" Press release for the Urban League and NAACP, n.d., in Local 11 Records, Healey Library Archives, quoted in ibid., p. 246.

136 "Both company and union" Jim Bollen quoted in Roboff, *Boston's Labor Movement*, p. 63.

136 "blacks didn't have much confidence" Coats, in "Glory Days" video, quoted in Bollen and Green, "The Long Strike," p. 257.

Chapter 15. Public Employees Organize

139 "the best union contract" Roland Messier quoted in Jim Bollen, "Council 93 History," n.p.

142 "from his soul" Mike Barnicle, *Boston Globe*, April 26, 1992.

Chapter 16: University Workers Adopt New Tactics

146 "no longer bought the myth" Public employee unionist quoted in Jacobs, "Rethinking Organized Labor."

149 "We don't want to seem" In *Organizing for the Union: A Publication of the B.U. Local of the District 65, UAW* (1983), p. 4, quoted in Lomasson, "'We Built the Union Ourselves,'" p. 62.

149 "There was real committed vision" Barbara Rahke interview, Feb. 21, 1991, in ibid., p. 63.

149 "looking back behind you" Ken Rosen interview, July 6, 1991, quoted in ibid., p. 65.

151 "The meetings around negotiations" Carol Gabin interview, June 4, 1991, in ibid., p. 60.

151 "Our union believes in" Ferd Wulkan, personal files, 1983–1988, in ibid., p. 57.

151 "stand up for herself" Beth Morrison interview, June 13, 1991, in ibid., p. 67.

152 "internalize a certain amount" Joan Bailey interview, Feb. 25, 1991, in ibid., p. 71.

152 "That's how I learned to think" Morrison interview, in ibid., p. 102.

Chapter 17: Protecting Health and Safety

157 "at least 390,000 new cases" 1972 presidential report quoted in Daniel M. Berman, "Death on the Job," p. 44.

158 "It seemed that for the first time" *Live Wire* (Utility Workers Local 369), Summer 1986, p. 15.

158 "We are returning to work" Joseph Faherty, "Special

Strike Issue," *Live Wire* (Utility Workers Local 369), Summer 1986.

159 "to visit the factory and discover the truth" Gabriel García quoted in Victoria Martinez, Testimony before United States Congress Senate Committee on Labor and Human Resources, Oct. 29, 1992, pp. 1–2, 4–5.

160 "Massachusetts" From "We Ain't Gonna Give It Back" CD or tape, John O'Connor, P.O. Box 582, Greenfield, Mass 01302.

161 "Death in the workplace" Nancy Lessin, in "Testimony on the Comprehensive Occupational Safety and Health Act (HR 1280)," *New Solutions* (Winter 1994): 83.

161 "The unforgettable lesson" Nancy Lessin, in Testimony before United States Congress Senate Committee on Labor and Human Resources, Oct. 29, 1991, p. 8.

162 "credit for this conviction" Nancy Lessin, in *Boston Globe*, March 18, 1994.

162 "Today in Massachusetts" Lessin, in "Testimony on the Comprehensive Occupational Safety and Health Reform Act," p. 85.

162 "Productivity and competitiveness" Ibid., p. 83.

Chapter 18: Massachusetts Building Trades Fight Back

164 "set a precedent" *New England Real Estate Journal*, June 24, 1988, quoted in Erlich, *Labor at the Ballot Box*, p. 8.

164 "We were pretty depressed" Joe Dart quoted in Erlich, *Labor at the Ballot Box*, pp. 56–57.

164 "Our failure scared us" Rich Gambino quoted in ibid., p. 57

165 "We obviously needed the money" Ibid., p. 62.

165 "What we found was amazing" Russ Sheehan quoted in ibid., pp. 65–66.

165 "Doing voter registration introduced me" Rick Brown quoted in ibid., p. 71.

167 "only clear result" Data Resources, Inc., "Study of the Economic Impact of Repeal of the Massachusetts Prevailing Wage Law," Aug. 18, 1988, quoted in ibid., p. 77.

168 "Pioneering" Copyright 1986 by Susan Eisenberg, reprinted by permission. From *Radical America* 23, nos. 2 and 3, and reprinted in *Tradeswomen Magazine*, *Midwest Labor Review,* and *Harvard Women's Law Review*. Included in NOT on a SILVER PLATTER (mixed media installation).

169 "Many of the municipal workers" Richard Boutiette quoted in ibid., p. 92.

169 "When our workers were appealed to" and "You just mentioned" Nancy Mills quoted in ibid., pp. 94, 95.

170 "How do you build" Tom Cunha in *Boston Ledger*, Sept. 30, 1988, quoted in ibid., p. 105.

170 "ironic that as the construction trades" Molly Yard in Committee on Quality of Life quote sheet, quoted in ibid., p. 112.

170 "the devastating impact" Augusto Grace to Arthur Osborn, Oct. 21, 1988, quoted in ibid., p. 119.

170 "Question 2 was placed" Cesar Chavez to UFW supporters in Massachusetts, Oct. 6, 1988, quoted in ibid., p. 119.

170 Robert Haynes All quotes from interview with Tom Juravich on February 14, 1996.

172 "They mobilized themselves" Janice Fine quoted in ibid., p. 168.

172 "Democracy in our unions" Jack Getchell quoted in ibid., p. 207.

172 "can't do it alone" Robert Haynes quoted in ibid., p. 204.

172 "the labor movement will arrest its decline" Mark Erlich quoted in ibid., p. 205.

Sources

Adamic, Louis. *My America, 1928–1938.* New York: Harpers, 1938.

AFL-CIO Committee on the Evolution of Work. *The Changing Situation of Workers and Their Unions.* Washington, D.C.: AFL-CIO, 1985.

Amalgamated Transit Union Staff. *A History of the Amalgamated Transit Union.* Washington, D.C.: Amalgamated Transit Union, 1992.

Banks, Ann, ed. *First-Person America.* New York: Knopf, 1982.

Barnicle, Mike. "Our Benefit, Their Sacrifice." *Boston Globe,* April 26, 1992.

Bartlett, Donald L., and James B. Steele. *America: What Went Wrong?* Kansas City: Andrews and McMeel, 1992.

Beatty, Jack. *The Rascal King: The Life and Times of James Michael Curley.* Reading: Addison Wesley, 1992.

Bedford, Henry F. *Socialism and the Workers in Massachusetts, 1896–1912.* Amherst: University of Massachusetts Press, 1966.

———, ed. *Their Lives and Their Numbers: The Condition of Working People in Massachusetts, 1870–1900.* Ithaca: Cornell University Press, 1995.

Berman, Daniel M. *Death on the Job: Occupational Health and Safety Struggles in the United States.* New York: Monthly Review Press, 1978.

Bernstein, Irving. *The Lean Years: A History of the American Worker.* Boston: Houghton Mifflin, 1960.

———. *The Turbulent Years: A History of the American Worker, 1933–1941.* Boston: Houghton Mifflin, 1970.

Blewett, Mary H. *The Last Generation: Work and Life in the Textile Mills of Lowell, Massachusetts, 1910–1960.* Amherst: University of Massachusetts Press, 1990.

———. *Men, Women, and Work: Class, Gender, and Protest in the New England Shoe Industry, 1879–1910.* Urbana: University of Illinois Press, 1988.

———. *We Will Rise in Our Might: Workingwomen's Voices from Nineteenth-Century New England.* Ithaca: Cornell University Press, 1991.

———, ed. *Surviving Hard Times: The Working People of Lowell.* Lowell, Mass.: Museum of American Textile History, 1982.

Blodgett, Geoffrey. *The Gentle Reformers: Massachusetts Democrats in the Cleveland Era.* Cambridge: Harvard University Press, 1966.

Bluestone, Barry, and Bennett Harrison. *The Deindustrialization of America: Plant Closings, Community Abandonment, and the Dismantling of Basic Industry.* New York: Basic Books, 1982.

Bollen, James. "Council 93 History." Manuscript for AFSCME Council 93 in Boston (1986).

Bollen, Jim, and Jim Green. "The Long Strike: The Practice of Solidarity among Boston's Packinghouse Workers." In *Labor in Massachusetts: Selected Essays,* ed. Kenneth Fones-Wolf and Martin Kaufman. Westfield: Institute for Massachusetts Studies, 1990.

Bollen, Jim, and Steve Miller. *The Colonial Strike.* Boston: Boston Community School, 1973.

Bollen, Peter, *A Handbook of Great Labor Quotations.* Lynnfield, Mass.: Hillside Books, 1983.

Bolster, W. Jeffrey. "'To Feel Like a Man': Black Seamen in the Northern States." *Journal of American History* 76 (March 1990): 1173–99.

Bonislawski, Michael. "The Anti-Communist Movement and Industrial Unionism: IUE vs. UE." Masters' Thesis, American Studies Program, University of Massachusetts at Boston, 1992.

Boston Carmen's Local 589. *Seventy-Fifth Anniversary Booklet.* Boston: Amalgamated Transit Union Local 589, 1987.

Brecher, Jeremy, and Tim Costello, eds. *Building Bridges: The Emerging Grassroots Coalition of Labor and Community.* New York: Monthly Review Press, 1990.

Bronfenbrenner, Kate. "Seeds of Resurgence: Successful Union Strategies for Winning Certification and First Contracts in the 1980s and Beyond." Ph.D. Dissertation, Cornell University, 1993.

Bronfenbrenner, Kate, and Tom Juravich. "Seeds of Resurgence: The Promise of Organizing in the Public and Private Sectors." Working Paper of the Institute for the Study of Labor Organizations, Washington, D.C., 1994.

Brooks, Thomas R. *Toil and Trouble: A History of American Labor.* New York: Delta, 1964.

Cameron, Ardis. "Bread and Roses Revisited: Women's Culture and Working Class Activism in the Lawrence Strike of 1912."

In *Women, Work and Protest: A Century of U.S. Women's Labor History*, ed. Ruth Milkman. London: Routledge, 1985.

———. *Radicals of the Worst Sort: Laboring Women in Lawrence, Massachusetts, 1860–1912*. Urbana: University of Illinois Press, 1993.

Clark, Christopher, *The Communitarian Moment: The Radical Challenge of the Northampton Association*. Ithaca: Cornell University Press, 1995.

Cohen, Bruce. "Worcester, Open Shop City." In *Labor in Massachusetts: Selected Essays*, ed. Kenneth Fones-Wolf and Martin Kaufman. Westfield: Westfield State College, 1990.

Cole, Donald B. *Immigrant City: Lawrence, Massachusetts, 1845–1912*. Chapel Hill: University of North Carolina Press, 1963.

Commons, John R., et al., eds. *A Documentary History of American Industrial Society*. 10 vols. Cleveland: Arthur H. Clark Company, 1910.

Cumbler, John T. *Working Class Community in Industrial America: Work, Leisure, and Struggle in Two Industrial Cities, 1880–1930*. Westport, Conn.: Greenwood Press, 1979.

Curley, James Michael. *I'd Do It Again: A Record of All My Uproarious Years*. Englewood Cliffs, N.J.: Prentice Hall, 1957.

Dawley, Alan. *Class and Community: The Industrial Revolution in Lynn*. Cambridge: Harvard University Press, 1976.

Douglass, Frederick. *The Life and Times of Frederick Douglass, Written by Himself*. Hartford: Park Publishing, 1891.

Dublin, Thomas. *Women at Work: The Transformation of Work and Community in Lowell, Massachusetts, 1826–1860*. New York: Columbia University Press, 1979.

———, ed. *Farm to Factory; Women's Letters, 1830–1860*. New York: Columbia University Press, 1981.

Dubofsky, Melvyn. *We Shall Be All: A History of the Industrial Workers of the World*. New York: Quadrangle, 1969.

Eisler, Benita, ed. *The Lowell Offering: Writings by New England Mill Women (1840–1845)*. Philadelphia: J.B. Lippincott Company, 1977.

Erlich, Mark. *Labor at the Ballot Box: The Massachusetts Prevailing Wage Campaign of 1988*. Philadelphia: Temple University Press, 1990.

———. *With Our Hands: The Story of Carpenters in Massachusetts*. Philadelphia: Temple University Press, 1986.

"The Faces and Voices of the Massachusetts Teachers Association." Boston: Massachusetts Teachers Association, 1995.

Faler, Paul. *Mechanics and Manufacturers in the Early Industrial Revolution: Lynn, Massachusetts, 1780–1860*. Albany: State University of New York Press, 1981.

Fenton, Edwin. *Immigrants and Unions: Italians and American Labor, 1870–1920*. New York: Arno Press, 1975.

Fink, Gary M. *Biographical Directory of American Labor Leaders*. Vol. 1. Westport, Conn.: Greenwood Press, 1974.

Flexner, Eleanor. *Century of Struggle: The Women's Rights Movement in the United States*. Cambridge: Harvard University Press, 1959.

Foner, Philip S. *The Fur and Leather Workers Union*. Newark: Nordan Press, 1950.

———. *The History of the American Labor Movement from the Founding of the American Federation of Labor to the Emergence of American Imperialism*. New York: International Publishers, 1955.

———. *The History of the Labor Movement in the United States: From Colonial Times to the Founding of the American Federation of Labor*. New York: International Publishers, 1947.

———. *Organized Labor and the Black Worker, 1619–1981*. New York: International Publishers, 1981.

———. "A Voice for Equality: *Boston Daily Evening Voice*, 1864–1867." *Science and Society* 38 (1974): 304–25.

———. *Women and the American Labor Movement: From Colonial Times to the Eve of World War I*. New York: Free Press, 1979.

———, ed. *The Factory Girls: A Collection of Writings*. Urbana: University of Illinois Press, 1977.

———, ed. *We the Other People: Alternative Declarations of Independence by Labor Groups, Farmers, Women's Rights Advocates, Socialists, and Blacks, 1829–1975* Urbana: University of Illinois Press, 1976.

Forant, Robert. "Union Activity in the Springfield Area, 1933–1945." Manuscript.

Frankfurter, Felix. *The Case of Sacco and Vanzetti: A Critical Analysis for Lawyers and Laymen*. Boston: Little, Brown, 1927.

Garraty, John A., ed. *Labor and Capital in the Gilded Age: Testimony Taken by the Senate Committee upon the Relations between Labor and Capital-1883*. Boston: Little, Brown, 1968.

Gelbspan, Ross, and Jonathan Kaufman. "Blacks Faring Better in Trade Unions Than on Campuses." *Boston Globe*, November 11, 1985.

Georgianna, Daniel, and Roberta Hazen Aaronson. *The Strike of '28*. New Bedford: Spinner Publications, 1993.

Goldberg, David J. *A Tale of Three Cities: Labor Organization and Protest in Paterson, Passaic, and Lawrence, 1916–1921*. New Brunswick, N.J.: Rutgers University Press, 1989.

Gooding, Cheryl, and Patricia Reeve. "Coalition Building for

Community-Based Labor Education." *Policy Studies Journal* 18, no. 2 (Winter 1989–90).

Gooding, James Henry. *On the Altar of Freedom: A Black Soldier's Civil War Letters from the Front*, ed. Virginia Matzke Adams. Amherst: University of Massachusetts Press, 1991.

Green, Constance McLaughlin. *The Role of Women as Production Workers in War Plants in the Connecticut Valley*. In *Smith College Studies in History* 28 (1946).

Green, James R. *The World of the Worker: Labor in Twentieth Century America*. New York: Hill and Wang, 1980.

Green, James R., and Hugh Carter Donahue. *Boston's Workers: A Labor History*. Boston: Boston Public Library, 1979.

Green, James, and Robert Hayden. "A. Philip Randolph and Boston's African-American Railroad Workers." *Trotter Review* 6, no. 1 (1992).

Green, James, and Chris Tilly. "Service Unionism: New Directions for Organizing." *Labor Law Journal* (August 1987).

Gross, Laurence F. *The Course of Industrial Decline: The Booth Cotton Mills of Lowell, Massachusetts, 1835–1955*. Baltimore: Johns Hopkins University Press, 1993.

Halter, Marilyn. "The Cape Verdeans" and "The Labor Strike of 1933." In *Cranberry Harvest: A History of Cranberry Growing in Massachusetts*, ed. Joseph D. Thomas. New Bedford: Spinner Publications, 1990.

Handlin, Oscar. *Boston's Immigrants: A Study in Acculturation*. Cambridge: Harvard University Press, 1941.

Harris, William H. *Keeping the Faith: A. Phillip Randolph, Milton Webster and the Brotherhood of Sleeping Car Porters, 1925–37*. Urbana: University of Illinois Press, 1991.

Hartford, William. "Unions, Labor Markets and Deindustrialization: The Holyoke Textile Industry." In *Labor in Massachusetts: Selected Essays*, ed. Kenneth Fones-Wolf and Martin Kaufman. Westfield: Institute for Massachusetts Studies, 1990.

———. *Where Is Our Responsibility? Unions and Economic Change in the New England Textile Industry, 1870–1960*. Amherst: University of Massachusetts Press, in press.

———. *Working People of Holyoke: Class and Ethnicity in a Massachusetts Mill Town, 1850–1960*. New Brunswick, N.J.: Rutgers University Press, 1990.

Hartz, Louis. "Seth Luther: The Story of a Working-Class Rebel." *New England Quarterly* 13 (September 1940): 401–18.

Heintz, Albert M., and John R. Whitney. *History of the Massachusetts State Federation of Labor, 1887–1935*. Worcester: Labor News, 1935.

Hoerder, Dirk. "Boston Leaders, Boston Crowds." In *The American Revolution: Explorations in the History of American Radicalism*, ed. Alfred Young. DeKalb: Northern Illinois University Press, 1974.

Hoerr, John. "Organizing in a Different Voice: The Harvard of the Labor Movement." *The American Prospect* (Summer 1993).

Houndshell, David A. *From the American System to Mass Production, 1800–1932*. Baltimore: Johns Hopkins University Press, 1984.

Huston, James L. "Facing an Angry Labor: The American Public Interprets the Shoemaker Strike of 1860." *Civil War History* 28 (September 1982): 197–212.

Hyman, Collette A. "Labor Organizing and Female Institution Building: The Chicago Women's Trade Union League, 1904–24." In *Women, Work and Protest: A Century of U.S. Women's Labor History*, ed. Ruth Milkman. London: Routledge, 1985.

Jackson, Brian. *The Black Flag: A Look Back at the Strange Case of Nicola Sacco and Bartolomeo Vanzetti*. Boston: Routledge, 1981.

Jacobs, Sally. "Rethinking Organized Labor." *New England Business*, October 3, 1983.

Johnson, Ethel M. "Labor Progress in Boston, 1880–1930." In *Fifty Years of Boston: A Memorial Volume*, ed. Elisabeth M. Herlihy. Boston: Goodspeeds Bookstore, 1937.

Josephson, Hannah. *The Golden Threads: New England's Mill Girls and Magnates*. 1949. Reprint, New York: Russell and Russell, 1967.

Juravich, Tom. *Chaos on the Shop Floor: A Worker's View of Quality, Productivity and Management*. Philadelphia: Temple University Press, 1985.

Keyssar, Alex. *Out of Work: The First Century of Unemployment in Massachusetts*. Cambridge: Cambridge University Press, 1986.

Kornbluh, Joyce L. *Rebel Voices: An I.W.W. Anthology*. Ann Arbor: University of Michigan Press, 1964.

Laurie, Bruce. *From Artisan to Worker: Labor in Nineteenth-Century America*. New York: Hill and Wang, 1989.

———. *Working People of Philadelphia, 1800–1850*. Philadelphia: Temple University Press, 1980.

Lazerow, Jama. "'The Workingman's Hour': The 1886 Labor Uprising in Boston." *Labor History* 21, no. 2 (Spring 1980): 200–221.

Lepore, Jill. "Resistance, Reform, and Repression: Italian Immigrant Laborers in Clinton, 1896–1906." In *Labor in Massachusetts: Selected Essays*, ed. Kenneth Fones-Wolf and Martin Kaufman. Westfield: Westfield State College, 1990.

Lessin, Nancy, and Charley Richardson. "COSHes Help Build Healthy Unions." *Labor Research and Review* 16 (Fall 1990): 75–82.

Levine, Susan. *Labor's True Woman: Carpet Weavers, Industrialization, and Labor Reform in the Gilded Age.* Philadelphia: Temple University Press, 1984.

Levy, Leonard. *The Law of the Commonwealth and Chief Justice Shaw.* 1957. Reprint, New York: Oxford University Press, 1987.

Lomasson, Leslie A. "'We Built the Union Ourselves': A Feminist Model of Unionism." M.A. thesis, Labor Relations and Research Center, University of Massachusetts at Amherst, 1994.

Luther, Seth. *An Address to the Working-Men of New England on the State of Education and on the Condition of the Producing Classes in Europe and America.* Boston: Published by the Author, 1832.

McFeely, William S. *Frederick Douglass.* New York: W. W. Norton, 1991.

McNeill, George E., ed. *The Labor Movement: The Problem of Today.* Boston: A. M. Bridgman, 1886.

Mann, Arthur. *Yankee Reformers in the Urban Age.* Cambridge, Mass.: Belknap Press, 1954.

Manning, Seaton Wesley. "Negro Trade Unionists in Boston." *Social Forces* 17 (December 1938).

Massachusetts History Workshop. *They Can't Run the Office without Us: Sixty Years of Office Work in Boston.* Boston: Red Sun Press, 1985.

Matles, James, and James Higgins. *Them and Us: Struggles of a Rank-and-File Union.* New York: Prentice-Hall, 1974.

Melville, Herman. *Moby Dick.* New York: Oxford Press, 1983.

Miernyk, William D. *Inter-Industry Labor Mobility: The Case of the New England Textile Worker.* Boston: Northeastern University Press, 1955.

Milkman, Ruth. *Gender at Work: The Dynamics of Job Segregation by Sex during World War II.* Urbana: University of Illinois Press, 1987.

Miller, Marc Scott. *The Irony of Victory: World War II and Lowell, Massachusetts.* Urbana: University of Illinois Press, 1988.

Mitchell, Brian C. *The Paddy Camps: The Irish of Lowell, 1821–1861.* Urbana: University of Illinois Press, 1988.

Montgomery, David. *Beyond Equality: Labor and the Radical Republicans, 1862–1872.* New York: Knopf, 1967.

———. *Citizen Worker: The Experience of Workers in the United States with Democracy and the Free Market during the Nine-*

teenth *Century.* Cambridge: Cambridge University Press, 1991.

———. *Workers' Control in America: Studies in the History of Work, Technology and Labor Struggles.* Cambridge: Cambridge University Press, 1977.

Moody, Kim. *An Injury to All: The Decline of American Unionism.* New York: Verso, 1988.

Morris, Richard B. *Government and Labor in Early America.* New York: Columbia University Press, 1946.

———, ed. *The American Worker.* Washington, D.C.: U.S. Government Printing Office, 1976.

Murphy, Marjorie. *Blackboard Unions: The AFT and the NEA, 1900–1980.* Ithaca: Cornell University Press, 1990.

Murphy, Teresa Anne. *Ten Hours' Labor: Religion, Reform, and Gender in Early New England.* Ithaca: Cornell University Press, 1992.

Nash, June C. *From Tank Town to High Tech: The Clash of Community and Industrial Cycles.* Albany: State University of New York Press, 1989.

Needleman, Ruth. "Women Workers: A Force for Rebuilding Unionism." *Labor Research Review* 11 (Spring 1988): 1–13.

Nelson, James. *The Mine Workers' District 50: The Story of the Gas, Coke, and Chemical Unions of Massachusetts and Their Growth into a National Union.* New York: Exposition Press, 1955.

Norkunas, Martha. "'He Has to Be a Learned Man': Workers' Culture at the Heywood-Wakefield Company, 1935–1979." In *Shifting Gears* pamphlet series published by the Massachusetts Foundation for the Humanities and Public Policy.

Norwood, Stephen H. *Labor's Flaming Youth: Telephone Operators and Worker Militancy, 1878–1923.* Urbana: University of Illinois Press, 1990.

"Organizing for Health and Safety." *Labor Research Review* (Fall 1990).

Palladino, Grace. *Dreams of Dignity, Workers of Vision: A History of the International Brotherhood of Electrical Workers.* Washington, D.C.: International Brotherhood of Electrical Workers, 1991.

Pesotta, Rose. *Bread upon the Waters.* New York: Dodd and Mead, 1945.

Pessen, Edward. *Most Uncommon Jacksonians: The Radical Leaders of the Early Labor Movement.* Albany: State University of New York Press, 1967.

Phillips, Susan, Sandy Felder, and Fred Trusten. "Local 509 Turns Thirty: A Brief History of Local 509." Manuscript for SEIU Local 509 in Boston (1991).

Prude, Jonathan. *The Coming of Industrial Order: The Town and*

Factory Life in Rural Massachusetts, 1810–1860. New York: Cambridge University Press, 1983.

Putney, Martha S. *Black Sailors: Afro-American Merchant Seamen and Whalemen prior to the Civil War.* Westport, Conn.: Greenwood Press, 1987.

Robinson, Harriet H. *Loom and Spindle: or, Life among the Early Mill Girls.* 1898. Reprint, Kailua, Hawaii: Press Pacifica, 1976.

Roboff, Sari. *Boston's Labor Movement: An Oral History of Work and Organizing.* Boston: Boston 200, 1977.

Roediger, David R., and Philip S. Foner. *Our Own Time: A History of American Labor and the Working Day.* Westport, Conn.: Greenwood Press, 1989.

Romer, Sam. *The International Brotherhood of Teamsters.* New York: Wiley, 1962.

Rosenzweig, Roy. *Eight Hours for What We Will: Workers and Leisure in an Industrial City, 1870–1920.* Cambridge: Cambridge University Press, 1983.

Russell, Francis. *A City in Terror—1919—The Boston Police Strike.* New York: Viking, 1975.

Silva, Philip, Jr. "Robert Howard, Labor Leader." *Spinner* (New Bedford, Mass.) 3 (1984): 142–45.

Spaulding, Robert V. "The Boston Mercantile Community and the Promotion of the Textile Industry in New England, 1813–1860." Ph.D. diss., Yale University, 1963.

Stein, Leon, and Philip Taft, eds. *Religion, Reform, and Revolution: Labor Panaceas in the Nineteenth Century.* New York: Arno Press, 1969.

Tax, Meredith. *The Rising of the Women: Feminist Solidarity and Class Conflict, 1880–1917.* New York: Monthly Review Press, 1980.

Tepperman, Jean. *Not Servants, Not Machines: Office Workers Speak Out.* Boston: Beacon Press, 1976.

"Testimony on the Comprehensive Occupational Safety and Health Reform Act (HR 1280)." *New Solutions* (Winter 1994).

Tomlins, Christopher L. "AFL Unions in the 1930s: Their Performance in Historical Perspective." *Journal of American History* 65 (March 1979): 1021–42.

———. *Law, Labor, and Ideology in the Early American Republic.* New York: Cambridge University Press, 1993.

———. *The State and the Unions: Labor Relations, Law, and the Organized Labor Movement in America, 1880–1960.* Cambridge: Cambridge University Press, 1985.

Torres, Andres. "Latinos and Labor: Challenges and Opportunities." *New England Journal of Public Policy* 11, no. 1 (Spring-Summer 1995): 147–160.

Trout, Charles H. *Boston, The Great Depression and the New Deal.* New York: Oxford University Press, 1977.

U.S. House of Representatives. *The Strikes at Lawrence: Hearings before the Committee on Rules of the House of Representatives on Resolutions 409 and 433.* 62nd Cong., 2nd sess. Washington, D.C.: U.S. Government Printing Office, 1912.

U.S. Immigration Commission. *Immigrants in Industries: Woolen and Worsted Goods Manufacturing.* 61st Cong., 2nd sess., part 4. Washington, D.C.: U.S. Government Printing Office, 1911.

Voss, Kim. *The Making of American Exceptionalism: The Knights of Labor and Class Formation in the Nineteenth Century.* Ithaca: Cornell University Press, 1993.

Ware, Caroline. *The Early New England Cotton Manufacture: A Study in Industrial Beginnings.* Boston: Houghton Mifflin, 1931.

Ware, Norman. *The Industrial Worker, 1840–1860.* 1924. Reprint, Chicago: Quadrangle Books, 1964.

Wertheimer, Barbara Mayer. *We Were There: The Story of Working Women in America.* New York: Pantheon, 1977.

Wilentz, Sean. *Chants Democratic: New York City and the Rise of the American Working Class, 1788–1850.* New York: Oxford University Press, 1984.

Wise, Nancy Baker, and Christy Wise. *A Mouthful of Rivets: Women at Work in World War II.* San Francisco: Jossey-Baker, 1994.

Withorn, Ann. *The Circle Game: Services for the Poor in Massachusetts, 1966–1978.* Amherst: University of Massachusetts Press, 1982.

"Women's Ways of Organizing: A Conversation with AFSCME Organizers Kris Rondeau and Gladys McKenzie." *Labor Research Review* 18 (Fall–Winter 1991–92): 45–59.

Woods, Robert, ed. *The City Wilderness: A Settlement Study.* Boston: Houghton Mifflin, 1898.

Zonderman, David A. *Aspirations and Anxieties: New England Workers and the Mechanized Factory System, 1815–1850.* New York: Oxford University Press, 1992.

Commonwealth of Toil Advisory Board

Patricia Reeve, Labor Studies Program
University of Massachusetts Boston

Bruce Laurie, History Department
University of Massachusetts Amherst

Mary Blewett, History Department
University of Massachusetts Lowell

Ardis Cameron, History Department
University of Southern Maine

Phillip Sylvia, History Department
Bridgewater State College

Sue Porter Benson, History Department
University of Connecticut

Marty Blatt
Lowell National Historical Park

Mark Erlich
Carpenters Local 40

Maynard Seider, Sociology Department
North Adams State College

Ken Fones-Wolf, Center for Labor Studies
West Virginia University

Robert Haynes
Massachusetts AFL-CIO

Patricia Greenfield, Labor Relations and Research Center
University of Massachusetts Amherst

José Soler, Labor Education Center
University of Massachusetts Dartmouth

Dan Georgiana, Economics Department
University of Massachusetts Dartmouth

Illustration Sources

Chapter 1

Pages 4, 6–7, 8, and 10: University of Massachusetts, Lowell, Center for Lowell History [6–7: Locks and Canals Collection]

Chapter 2

Page 12: Society for the Preservation of New England Antiquities; 13: Horace Greeley et al., *Great Industries of the United States, . . .* (Hartford, 1871); 15: Metropolitan Museum of Art (all rights reserved), gift of I. N. Phelps Stokes, Edward S. Hawes, Alice Mary Hawes, Marion Hawes, 1938; 17: Sophia Smith Collection, Smith College

Chapter 3

Page 22: University of Massachusetts, Lowell, Center for Lowell History; 23: Society for the Preservation of New England Antiquities, photograph by Frederick J. Needham, late 1880s

Chapter 4

Page 29: Sophia Smith Collection, Smith College; 31, 32–33, 34, and 35: Old Dartmouth Historical Society—New Bedford Whaling Museum [31: photograph by Edmund Ashley; 32–33: photograph by Captain Henry Mandley; 34: photograph by Clifford W. Ashley; 35: photograph by Stephen F. Adams]

Chapter 5

Pages 39 and 43: Society for the Preservation of New England Antiquities, photographs by Keystone View Company, after 1910

Chapter 6

Pages 48–49, 50, 51, 52: Catholic University of America Archives, Terence Vincent Powderly Papers

Chapter 7

Pages 54, 56, and 58: State Historical Society of Wisconsin [54: negative # (X3) 50354; 56: negative # (X3) 50353; 58: negative # (X3) 50355]; 55 and 59: Special Collections and Archives, Records of the Massachusetts AFL-CIO, 1902–1995, W.E.B. Du Bois Library, University of Massachusetts, Amherst

Chapter 8

Page 61: Special Collections and Archives, Records of the Massachusetts AFL-CIO, 1902–1995, W.E.B. Du Bois Library, University of Massachusetts, Amherst; 62–63, 65, 66–67, and 68: Holyoke Public Library Corporation

Chapter 9

Pages 74, 77, and 78–79: Courtesy of Boston Public Library, Print Department, *Herald-Traveler* Collection [78–79: photograph by Paul A. Doherty]; 83 and 85: Collection of Immigrant City Archives, Lawrence, Massachusetts

Chapter 10

Pages 87, 88, 90, and 93: Courtesy of Boston Public Library, Print Department [87, 88, and 90: E.E. Bond Collection]; 94: Special Collections and Archives, Records of the Massachusetts AFL-CIO, 1902–1995, W.E.B. Du Bois Library, University of Massachusetts, Amherst

Chapter 11

Pages 98, 100, 102–3: Courtesy of Boston Public Library, Print Department [98: *Herald-Traveler* Collection; 100: photograph by Leslie Jones, 1921]; 105: University of Massachusetts, Lowell, Center for Lowell History

Chapter 12

Pages 107 and 108–9: Special Collections and Archives, W.E.B. Du Bois Library, University of Massachusetts, Amherst [107: Records of the Massachusetts AFL-CIO, 1902–1995; 108–9: Records of the Textile Workers of America, New Bedford Joint Board, 1939–1980]; 110 and 114–15: Courtesy of Boston Public Library, Print Department [110: *Herald-Traveler* Collection; 114–15: photograph by Leslie Jones]; 112: Chicago Historical Society

Chapter 13

Pages 121, 123, 124–25: Courtesy of Boston Public Library, Print Department [121: *Herald-Traveler* Collection; 123: Photograph by Maynard White]; 127: Special Collections and Archives, Records of the Textile Workers of America, New Bedford Joint

Board, 1939–1980, W.E.B. Du Bois Library, University of Massachusetts, Amherst

Chapter 14

Pages 131, 132, and 133: Special Collections and Archives, Records of the Textile Workers of America, New Bedford Joint Board, 1939–1980, W.E.B. Du Bois Library, University of Massachusetts, Amherst; 134: Archives and Special Collections Department, Healey Library, University of Massachusetts, Boston

Chapter 15

Pages 140–41 and 143: Courtesy of Boston Public Library, Print Department, *Herald-Traveler* Collection [143: photograph by Paul A. Doherty, April 1971]; 142 and 144: Susan Phillips

Chapter 16

Pages 146, 147, 149, and 150–51: Ferd Wulkan; 148: Women's Institute for Leadership Development

Chapter 17

Pages 156, 159, and 161: MassCOSH; 158: Massachusetts AFL-CIO

Chapter 18

Pages 163, 165, and 169: From Erlich, *Labor at the Ballot Box* [163: photograph by Martin Ploof; 165: photograph by Constance Thibaut; 169: photograph by John Gillooly]; 166: Special Collections and Archives, Records of the Massachusetts AFL-CIO, 1902–1995, W.E.B. Du Bois Library, University of Massachusetts, Amherst; 171: Massachusetts AFL-CIO

Index

DUE DATE